JUMBLE®
Magic

Puzzles to Mystify and Amaze!

Henri Arnold
and
Bob Lee

TRIUMPH
BOOKS

This book is available in quantity at special discounts
for your group or organization.

For further information, contact:

Triumph Books LLC
814 North Franklin Street
Chicago, Illinois 60610
Phone: (312) 337-0747
www.triumphbooks.com

Printed in U.S.A.

ISBN: 978-1-60078-795-9

Design by Sue Knopf

CONTENTS

Classic Puzzles

Daily Puzzles

Challenger Puzzles

Answers

JUMBLE

MAGIC

Classic Puzzles

JUMBLE®

Unscramble these four Jumbles, one letter to each square, to form four ordinary words.

ALLIC

UPASE

STERJE

LYKING

HOW SHE FELT WHEN SHE ARRIVED HOME AFTER A SHOPPING BINGE.

Now arrange the circled letters to form the surprise answer, as suggested by the above cartoon.

Print answer here ◯◯◯ " ◯◯◯◯◯◯ "

2

JUMBLE®

Unscramble these four Jumbles, one letter to each square, to form four ordinary words.

GROOF
◯◯ ◯◯

OMPET
◯◯◯

ATVARC
◯

ENCHIL
◯◯

You've had enough

BAR

WHAT KIND OF PLANS WAS THE ARCHITECT MAKING FOR HIM?

Now arrange the circled letters to form the surprise answer, as suggested by the above cartoon.

Print answer here ◯◯ ◯◯◯ ◯◯◯◯

JUMBLE®

Unscramble these four Jumbles, one letter to each square, to form four ordinary words.

TANBO

DANGL

CONARY

VAHLED

WAH!

WHAT NO UPRIGHT PERSON WOULD DO.

Now arrange the circled letters to form the surprise answer, as suggested by the above cartoon.

Print answer here

JUMBLE®

Unscramble these four Jumbles, one letter to
each square, to form four ordinary words.

PORRI

VUEMA

GROFTE

TUCLED

Famous philosopher

WORDS YOU MIGHT
GET FROM
VOLTAIRE.

Now arrange the circled letters to form
the surprise answer, as suggested by the
above cartoon.

Print answer here " ☐ ☐☐☐☐ ☐☐☐ "

JUMBLE®

Unscramble these four Jumbles, one letter to
each square, to form four ordinary words.

EUDES

SUGES

YAPNOC

DALLIP

Whew! That
was close!

DID HANGMEN
CARRY OUT SUCH
SENTENCES?

Now arrange the circled letters to form
the surprise answer, as suggested by the
above cartoon.

*Print answer
here* ◯◯◯◯◯◯◯◯◯◯ ONES

JUMBLE®

Unscramble these four Jumbles, one letter to each square, to form four ordinary words.

CEPEA

LYMAN

DILIOB

BYSMOL

Maybe he should see a shrink

HE COULDN'T REMEMBER—WHAT THIS WORD MEANT.

Now arrange the circled letters to form the surprise answer, as suggested by the above cartoon.

Print answer here "  "

7

JUMBLE®

Unscramble these four Jumbles, one letter to
each square, to form four ordinary words.

GEALE

VERAB

SMIDOH

UNGATH

WHAT YOU MIGHT
GET FROM A
DEBATER.

Now arrange the circled letters to form
the surprise answer, as suggested by the
above cartoon.

Print answer here "◯◯◯◯◯◯◯◯◯"

JUMBLE®

Unscramble these four Jumbles, one letter to each square, to form four ordinary words.

NOYOL

YICTH

STYJUL

LADRIA

HOW THEY BENT THEIR KNEES.

Now arrange the circled letters to form the surprise answer, as suggested by the above cartoon.

Print answer here " ☐☐☐☐☐ – ☐☐ "

9

JUMBLE®

Unscramble these four Jumbles, one letter to
each square, to form four ordinary words.

TOUHY

FRUOM

SITMIF

CACTEN

Work when
you please

A JOB FOR
SOMEONE WHO'S
WELL-PADDED.

Now arrange the circled letters to form
the surprise answer, as suggested by the
above cartoon.

Print answer here " ◯◯◯◯◯ "

JUMBLE®

Unscramble these four Jumbles, one letter to
each square, to form four ordinary words.

NERAV

VALIT

MEEGRE

SCIBEP

A FRUITFUL
SOURCE OF
INFORMATION.

Now arrange the circled letters to form
the surprise answer, as suggested by the
above cartoon.

*Print answer
here* THE ⭕⭕⭕⭕⭕⭕⭕⭕⭕⭕⭕

11

JUMBLE®

Unscramble these four Jumbles, one letter to
each square, to form four ordinary words.

NORPE

AVVLE

TRUFOH

SUCCAU

HOW THEY CLAPPED
THEIR HANDS WHEN
SHE SANG.

Now arrange the circled letters to form
the surprise answer, as suggested by the
above cartoon.

Print answer here ◯◯◯◯ THEIR ◯◯◯◯

JUMBLE®

Unscramble these four Jumbles, one letter to each square, to form four ordinary words.

ZIERP

CHALT

LETTOU

ABHORR

WHAT SHE HOPED THE BACHELOR WOULD DO ABOUT HIS WAY OF LIFE.

Now arrange the circled letters to form the surprise answer, as suggested by the above cartoon.

Print answer here " ☐☐☐☐☐ " ☐☐

JUMBLE®

Unscramble these four Jumbles, one letter to
each square, to form four ordinary words.

BEREM

LIDAP

TEENAG

GLEANT

WHAT HE HAD TO DO
EVERY TIME SHE HAD
AN ACCIDENT IN
THE KITCHEN.

Now arrange the circled letters to form
the surprise answer, as suggested by the
above cartoon.

Print answer here ◯◯◯ IT FOR ◯◯◯◯◯◯◯

JUMBLE®

Unscramble these four Jumbles, one letter to
each square, to form four ordinary words.

CARTT

HOOPT

TYMINE

BRUBUS

WHAT A SOAP OPERA
USUALLY IS.

Now arrange the circled letters to form
the surprise answer, as suggested by the
above cartoon.

Print answer here ☐☐☐☐ ON THE ☐☐☐

JUMBLE®

Unscramble these four Jumbles, one letter to
each square, to form four ordinary words.

LYDIO

NEESU

WREABE

ICKEOO

WHAT THE PRETTY
BLOND TEACHER WAS,
AS DESCRIBED BY
HER PUPILS.

Now arrange the circled letters to form
the surprise answer, as suggested by the
above cartoon.

Print answer here ◯◯◯◯◯ – ◯◯◯◯◯

JUMBLE®

Unscramble these four Jumbles, one letter to
each square, to form four ordinary words.

KARAP

FERIG

CENTEM

RYNTIG

WHAT'S THE BEST
AGE TO GET
HITCHED?

Now arrange the circled letters to form
the surprise answer, as suggested by the
above cartoon.

Print answer here " ⟨□□□□□⟩ - ⟨□□□⟩ "

JUMBLE®

Unscramble these four Jumbles, one letter to
each square, to form four ordinary words.

NOAPI

NIFET

TABEED

GUBBED

WHAT A PERSON
WHO CHEATS ON A
DIET IS APT
TO DO.

Now arrange the circled letters to form
the surprise answer, as suggested by the
above cartoon.

**Print
answer
here**

◯◯◯◯ — IN THE ◯◯◯

18

JUMBLE®

Unscramble these four Jumbles, one letter to
each square, to form four ordinary words.

LANUN

MUJOB

PUNACK

TONPHY

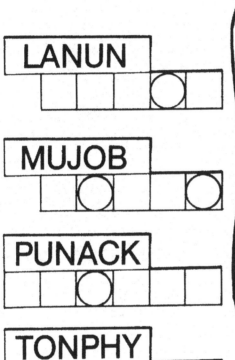

Sure, I'll lend
you the dough

WHAT AN HONEST
ELEVATOR MAN
PROBABLY IS.

Now arrange the circled letters to form
the surprise answer, as suggested by the
above cartoon.

Print answer here ☐☐ THE ☐☐ & ☐☐

JUMBLE®

Unscramble these four Jumbles, one letter to each square, to form four ordinary words.

SBELS

DYRIT

GRIFIN

RODINO

TONITE
JONES VS. SMITH

IN THIS SITUATION, YOU'LL BE VERY CLOSE TO A FIGHT.

Now arrange the circled letters to form the surprise answer, as suggested by the above cartoon.

Print answer here

20

JUMBLE®

Unscramble these four Jumbles, one letter to
each square, to form four ordinary words.

YACED

SHOIT

RAYATS

BARKEY

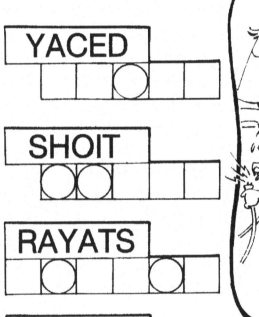

MIGHT BE
A CURRENT
SENSATION.

Now arrange the circled letters to form
the surprise answer, as suggested by the
above cartoon.

Print answer here

JUMBLE®

Unscramble these four Jumbles, one letter to
each square, to form four ordinary words.

EAZUG

TAWLZ

BELMIN

GUSINE

I told you he'd call back
if you just sat tight!

YOU NEED TO
BIDE YOUR TIME
TO PLAY THIS.

Now arrange the circled letters to form
the surprise answer, as suggested by the
above cartoon.

*Print
answer* THE ◯◯◯◯◯◯◯ ◯◯◯◯
here

JUMBLE®

Unscramble these four Jumbles, one letter to
each square, to form four ordinary words.

POCHE

RAHME

STEACK

UMSOQE

MADE AN IMPRESSION
ON THE BRIDLE
PATH.

Now arrange the circled letters to form
the surprise answer, as suggested by the
above cartoon.

Print answer here A ⬚⬚⬚⬚⬚⬚⬚⬚⬚⬚⬚

JUMBLE®

Unscramble these four Jumbles, one letter to each square, to form four ordinary words.

DYNOW

YORRS

STELED

TRYSAP

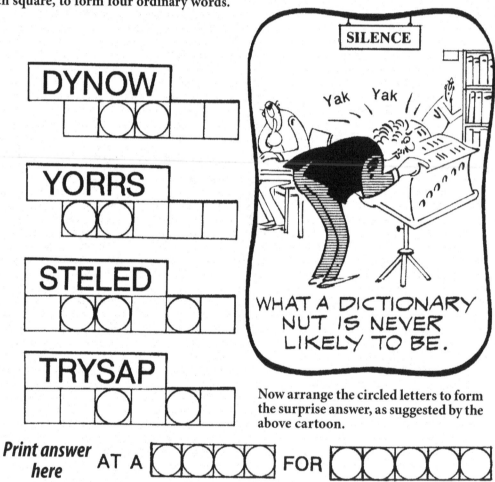

SILENCE

Yak   Yak

WHAT A DICTIONARY NUT IS NEVER LIKELY TO BE.

Now arrange the circled letters to form the surprise answer, as suggested by the above cartoon.

Print answer here AT A ⬡⬡⬡⬡ FOR ⬡⬡⬡⬡⬡

JUMBLE®

Unscramble these four Jumbles, one letter to each square, to form four ordinary words.

LEBER

VELGA

SOUTID

BRATIB

WHAT THEY SAID THE DYNAMITERS' ANNUAL SHINDIG WAS.

Now arrange the circled letters to form the surprise answer, as suggested by the above cartoon.

Print answer here A ☐☐☐☐☐ ☐☐☐☐☐

JUMBLE®

Unscramble these four Jumbles, one letter to
each square, to form four ordinary words.

GEGAU

CYKAT

QUORIL

VERABE

NO, HE WAS NOT
AFTER THE
FAMILY PET.

Now arrange the circled letters to form
the surprise answer, as suggested by the
above cartoon.

*Print answer
here* THE ⬡⬡⬡ ⬡⬡⬡⬡⬡⬡⬡⬡

JUMBLE®

MAGIC

Daily Puzzles

JUMBLE®

Unscramble these four Jumbles, one letter to
each square, to form four ordinary words.

LEERD

BLAWR

MURQUO

AURBUE

I'm getting hungry

COULD MAKE ONE
THINK OF FOOD—
A LINE OF MEN
WAITING FOR
HAIRCUTS.

Now arrange the circled letters to form
the surprise answer, as suggested by the
above cartoon.

Print
answer A "⬡⬡⬡⬡⬡⬡ ⬡⬡⬡⬡⬡"
here

JUMBLE®

Unscramble these four Jumbles, one letter to each square, to form four ordinary words.

LIBOR

HEWEL

CORNEE

MOTELE

WHAT THAT NEWCOMER MADE.

Now arrange the circled letters to form the surprise answer, as suggested by the above cartoon.

Print answer here " ☐☐☐ ☐☐☐☐☐ "

JUMBLE®

Unscramble these four Jumbles, one letter to
each square, to form four ordinary words.

CHUGO

ATING

LANNID

GLEIMN

THIS IS THE KEY
TO ALL GOOD
DRIVING.

Now arrange the circled letters to form
the surprise answer, as suggested by the
above cartoon.

Print answer here

JUMBLE®

Unscramble these four Jumbles, one letter to each square, to form four ordinary words.

DARAW

COUNE

GROHPE

NORBIN

MIGHT PROVIDE SOME REST FOR A TIRED FISH.

Now arrange the circled letters to form the surprise answer, as suggested by the above cartoon.

Print answer here THE ⬡⬡⬡⬡⬡⬡ ⬡⬡⬡

JUMBLE®

Unscramble these four Jumbles, one letter to
each square, to form four ordinary words.

WARFE

YAIRN

DURSTY

THORCC

DUE FOR A
"ROASTING" FROM
THE SERGEANT.

Now arrange the circled letters to form
the surprise answer, as suggested by the
above cartoon.

Print answer
here   A " ⬡⬡⬡ " ⬡⬡⬡⬡⬡⬡⬡

JUMBLE®

Unscramble these four Jumbles, one letter to
each square, to form four ordinary words.

FLAIN

KOWEA

PLOATS

LARREB

Don't believe a word of it

COULD BE THE
RESULT OF
SPINNING A LOT
OF TALES.

Now arrange the circled letters to form
the surprise answer, as suggested by the
above cartoon.

Print answer here A ☐☐☐☐ ☐☐ ☐☐☐☐☐

JUMBLE®

Unscramble these four Jumbles, one letter to each square, to form four ordinary words.

URFOL

RAALT

PELPIN

CINNEA

You're all in for a big surprise!

FOR SOMEONE WHO PLANS TO MAKE A SPLASH IN THE KITCHEN.

Now arrange the circled letters to form the surprise answer, as suggested by the above cartoon.

Print answer here

JUMBLE

Unscramble these four Jumbles, one letter to
each square, to form four ordinary words.

ROWBE

KNALF

RATHEG

DIFLED

Someday he'll own
the paper

STILL A STUDENT—
BUT HE HAS WITHIN
HIM THE ABILITY
TO MAKE MONEY.

Now arrange the circled letters to form
the surprise answer, as suggested by the
above cartoon.

Print answer here A " ☐ ☐ — ☐ ☐ ☐ ☐ ☐ ☐ "

JUMBLE®

Unscramble these four Jumbles, one letter to
each square, to form four ordinary words.

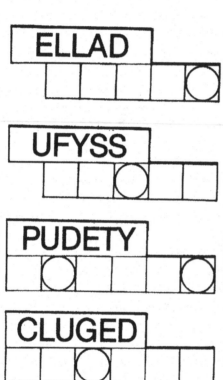

ELLAD

UFYSS

PUDETY

CLUGED

Get cleaned up—
we're expecting
company

HOW HE LOOKED
AFTER SPENDING
THE WHOLE DAY
PLANTING THE
GARDEN.

Now arrange the circled letters to form
the surprise answer, as suggested by the
above cartoon.

Print answer here "  "

JUMBLE®

Unscramble these four Jumbles, one letter to each square, to form four ordinary words.

TIPEY

HOTUM

WEENST

GRONTS

Time to put the light on

TO BE CONTINUED

IT'S SET TO LEAVE YOU IN THE DARK.

Now arrange the circled letters to form the surprise answer, as suggested by the above cartoon.

Print answer here

JUMBLE®

Unscramble these four Jumbles, one letter to
each square, to form four ordinary words.

NIGLY

SEERA

DELIRB

DULCED

OBVIOUSLY NOT A
FLY-BY-NIGHT.

Now arrange the circled letters to form
the surprise answer, as suggested by the
above cartoon.

*Print answer
here*   THE ⬡⬡⬡⬡⬡ ⬡⬡⬡⬡

JUMBLE®

Unscramble these four Jumbles, one letter to
each square, to form four ordinary words.

POATI

DESET

CUSSEN

ZERBAL

SUGGESTED THAT
HE WAS PROUD OF
THE FACT THAT HE
WORKED LESS THAN
ANYONE ELSE.

Now arrange the circled letters to form
the surprise answer, as suggested by the
above cartoon.

Print answer here AN ☐☐☐☐ ☐☐☐☐☐

JUMBLE

Unscramble these four Jumbles, one letter to
each square, to form four ordinary words.

SHECS

ROFEY

LUMUTT

JERPUM

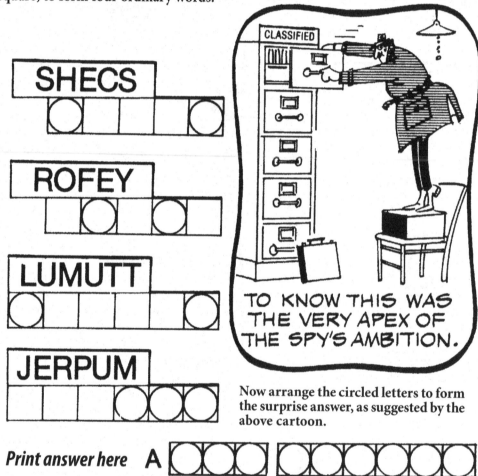

TO KNOW THIS WAS
THE VERY APEX OF
THE SPY'S AMBITION.

Now arrange the circled letters to form
the surprise answer, as suggested by the
above cartoon.

Print answer here A ⬚⬚⬚⬚ ⬚⬚⬚⬚⬚⬚

JUMBLE®

Unscramble these four Jumbles, one letter to
each square, to form four ordinary words.

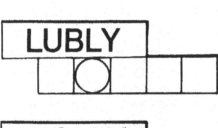

LUBLY

WOLLY

FARIDA

VELENE

THE SORT OF LIFE
YOU MIGHT EXPECT A
GLUTTON TO LEAD.

Now arrange the circled letters to form
the surprise answer, as suggested by the
above cartoon.

Print answer here A

JUMBLE®

Unscramble these four Jumbles, one letter to
each square, to form four ordinary words.

THACC

LIDAY

TURBAP

DEEMLY

WHERE'S THE MOST
DIFFICULT LOCK
TO PICK?

Now arrange the circled letters to form
the surprise answer, as suggested by the
above cartoon.

Print answer here   ON A ☐☐☐☐ ☐☐☐☐

JUMBLE®

Unscramble these four Jumbles, one letter to
each square, to form four ordinary words.

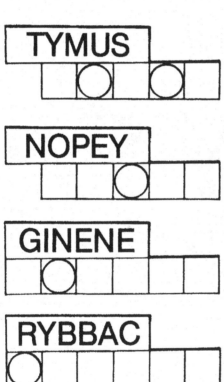

TYMUS

NOPEY

GINENE

RYBBAC

I hear he's a member
of the nobility

A TITLE THE
BOXER DIDN'T
AIM TO BE
OUT FOR.

Now arrange the circled letters to form
the surprise answer, as suggested by the
above cartoon.

Print answer here ""

JUMBLE®

Unscramble these four Jumbles, one letter to each square, to form four ordinary words.

SIPOE

DUNTE

CHOSOL

KRILLE

Oh, NOW I get it!

WHEN IS A JOKE MOST EFFECTIVE?

Now arrange the circled letters to form the surprise answer, as suggested by the above cartoon.

Print answer here

WHEN IT ⭕⭕⭕⭕⭕⭕⭕⭕ ⭕⭕⭕

JUMBLE®

Unscramble these four Jumbles, one letter to
each square, to form four ordinary words.

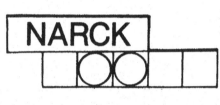

NARCK

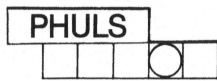

PHULS

TIXECE

UNCOBE

THE "DISINTE-
GRATION" OF ONE
STAR MAY THREATEN
THE WHOLE NATION.

Now arrange the circled letters to form
the surprise answer, as suggested by the
above cartoon.

Print answer here "  "

45

JUMBLE®

Unscramble these four Jumbles, one letter to
each square, to form four ordinary words.

SNALT

OOCCA

SWEDIT

THIMER

MOST DUELS ARE
RATHER SHORT
AFFAIRS BECAUSE
THEY ONLY
REQUIRE THIS.

Now arrange the circled letters to form
the surprise answer, as suggested by the
above cartoon.

Print answer here ☐☐☐ ☐☐☐☐☐☐☐

JUMBLE®

Unscramble these four Jumbles, one letter to
each square, to form four ordinary words.

VOFAR

NUEQE

LAIWHE

RETAIS

NOT A BAD
THING TO DO
WHEN IN COURT.

Now arrange the circled letters to form
the surprise answer, as suggested by the
above cartoon.

Print answer here

JUMBLE®

Unscramble these four Jumbles, one letter to
each square, to form four ordinary words.

GIREM

VANEH

TUFLAR

HUGNOE

WHAT WAS THE
NEW BRIDE'S
FAVORITE FISH?

Now arrange the circled letters to form
the surprise answer, as suggested by the
above cartoon.

Print answer here " ◯◯◯ – ◯◯◯◯ "

JUMBLE®

Unscramble these four Jumbles, one letter to
each square, to form four ordinary words.

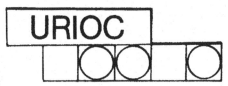

URIOC

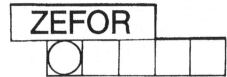

ZEFOR

DRAACE

NOLEST

Aha!

WHAT HE HAD ON
AS A RESULT OF
GETTING INTO A
PICKLE.

Now arrange the circled letters to form
the surprise answer, as suggested by the
above cartoon.

Print answer here A ⃝⃝⃝⃝ ⃝⃝⃝⃝

JUMBLE®

Unscramble these four Jumbles, one letter to
each square, to form four ordinary words.

REEMY

DRIPA

SLOIPH

CLEMPO

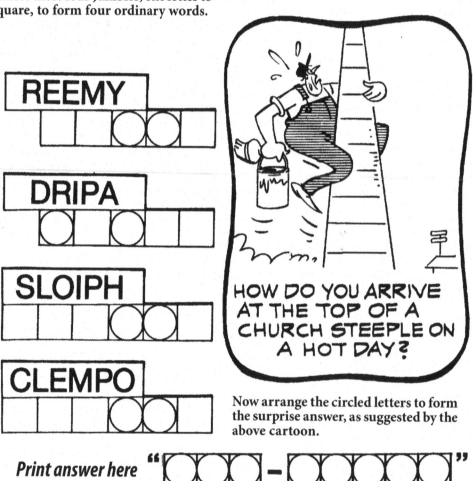

HOW DO YOU ARRIVE
AT THE TOP OF A
CHURCH STEEPLE ON
A HOT DAY?

Now arrange the circled letters to form
the surprise answer, as suggested by the
above cartoon.

Print answer here " ☐○○○☐ – ☐○○○○○☐ "

50

JUMBLE®

Unscramble these four Jumbles, one letter to
each square, to form four ordinary words.

AXORB

KEDAC

DUBACT

KUBECT

I told
you so

WHAT GARDENING
THAT BEGINS AT
DAYBREAK OFTEN
ENDS UP WITH.

Now arrange the circled letters to form
the surprise answer, as suggested by the
above cartoon.

Print answer here " ◯◯◯◯◯◯◯◯◯ "

JUMBLE.

Unscramble these four Jumbles, one letter to
each square, to form four ordinary words.

STRUY

COPAH

AJURAG

DUCINE

Must
be nuts!

CLICK!

WHAT PEOPLE
WHO CUT YOU SHORT
ON THE PHONE
EVIDENTLY HAVE.

Now arrange the circled letters to form
the surprise answer, as suggested by the
above cartoon.

Print answer here ⬡◯◯◯◯ − ◯◯◯

JUMBLE®

Unscramble these four Jumbles, one letter to
each square, to form four ordinary words.

DALGE

ATTIR

GORUME

CANVAT

A **GREAT OVEN** MIGHT PRODUCE MOST OF THIS.

Now arrange the circled letters to form
the surprise answer, as suggested by the
above cartoon.

Print answer
here " ⬡⬡⬡⬡⬡⬡⬡⬡⬡⬡⬡ "

JUMBLE®

Unscramble these four Jumbles, one letter to
each square, to form four ordinary words.

OVEEK

SHUBY

CEADED

KILLEY

VEGETABLES THAT
SOUND AS THOUGH
THEY SHOULD
NEVER BE SERVED
ABOARD SHIP.

Now arrange the circled letters to form
the surprise answer, as suggested by the
above cartoon.

Print answer here

JUMBLE®

Unscramble these four Jumbles, one letter to
each square, to form four ordinary words.

UNDAT

ORNOC

FINTEC

TULFAY

WHAT SOME
JOGGERS
TEND TO DO.

Now arrange the circled letters to form
the surprise answer, as suggested by the
above cartoon.

Print answer here ◯◯◯ ◯◯ ◯◯◯

JUMBLE®

Unscramble these four Jumbles, one letter to each square, to form four ordinary words.

LAIGY

YIHFS

KLEETT

MIRAPI

Looking forward to my first grandchild

WHEN THEY GOT MARRIED, THIS COULD HAVE BEEN THEIR "LIFE'S AIM."

Now arrange the circled letters to form the surprise answer, as suggested by the above cartoon.

Print answer here " ☐☐☐☐☐☐☐☐ "

JUMBLE®

Unscramble these four Jumbles, one letter to
each square, to form four ordinary words.

VOABE

KNACS

ENMURB

FUNIES

ME STUDIOS

I'm gonna
be a star

COULD BE THE RE-
SULT OF EVERYONE
WANTING TO GET
INTO THE ACT.

Now arrange the circled letters to form
the surprise answer, as suggested by the
above cartoon.

Print answer here A ⬡⬡⬡ ⬡⬡⬡⬡⬡

JUMBLE®

Unscramble these four Jumbles, one letter to
each square, to form four ordinary words.

ZYZID

RIQUE

RETAIW

UNRICH

A snap

WHAT A BRIGHT
STUDENT IS EXPECTED
TO DO WHEN
THERE'S AN EXAM.

Now arrange the circled letters to form
the surprise answer, as suggested by the
above cartoon.

Print
answer
here

○○○○ THROUGH THE ○○○○

JUMBLE

Unscramble these four Jumbles, one letter to each square, to form four ordinary words.

GULIE

NOANY

DIBORM

OOLANG

THIS MATERIAL NEVER GETS WORN OUT.

Now arrange the circled letters to form the surprise answer, as suggested by the above cartoon.

Print answer here

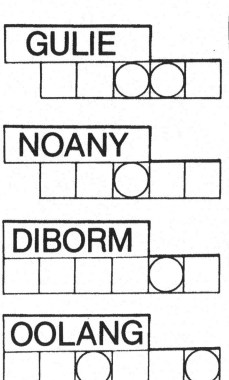

JUMBLE®

Unscramble these four Jumbles, one letter to
each square, to form four ordinary words.

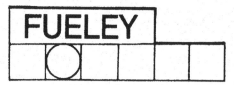

LIGUT

NULCE

DUNBOA

FUELEY

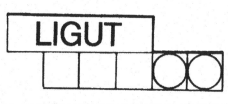

You're kind of old, aren't you?

ONE IS BEING POINTLESSLY FRANK WHEN SPEAKING THIS WAY.

Now arrange the circled letters to form
the surprise answer, as suggested by the
above cartoon.

Print answer here

60

JUMBLE®

Unscramble these four Jumbles, one letter to
each square, to form four ordinary words.

IBARR

SOGEO

FARFAY

GEDDUR

A BIG WHEEL IN
THE AMUSEMENT
BUSINESS.

Now arrange the circled letters to form
the surprise answer, as suggested by the
above cartoon.

Print answer here

61

JUMBLE®

Unscramble these four Jumbles, one letter to
each square, to form four ordinary words.

TCHEF

LATAN

NICCIP

DUNTIC

WHERE YOU'RE APT
TO FIND THE
MOST FISH.

Now arrange the circled letters to form
the surprise answer, as suggested by the
above cartoon.

Print answer here BETWEEN ◯◯◯◯◯ & ◯◯◯◯◯

JUMBLE®

Unscramble these four Jumbles, one letter to each square, to form four ordinary words.

INORM
⬜⬜◯◯⬜

ETTEW
⬜⬜◯⬜◯

GITSAM
◯⬜◯⬜⬜⬜

STUCCA
⬜⬜⬜◯⬜◯

QXXX-TV
W CASTING FOR
NEW SERIES

My uncle's
the producer

AN EASY WAY TO
GET ON TV.

Now arrange the circled letters to form the surprise answer, as suggested by the above cartoon.

Print answer here ◯◯◯ ◯◯ YOUR ◯◯◯

JUMBLE®

Unscramble these four Jumbles, one letter to
each square, to form four ordinary words.

LYRDY

SEBEO

VISWEL

VIRLED

YAK
YAK
YAK

WHAT'S A
PARROT?

Now arrange the circled letters to form
the surprise answer, as suggested by the
above cartoon.

Print
answer
here   A

JUMBLE®

Unscramble these four Jumbles, one letter to each square, to form four ordinary words.

PETIR

HORAC

BIRDHY

ROTTET

Can't it be turned off?

WHAT **THE RADIATOR** PRODUCED.

Now arrange the circled letters to form the surprise answer, as suggested by the above cartoon.

Print answer here "A ⬡⬡⬡⬡⬡⬡ ⬡⬡⬡⬡"

JUMBLE®

Unscramble these four Jumbles, one letter to
each square, to form four ordinary words.

LOCCI

OSKET

GUBLIN

NORIPS

WHAT THE
REFRIGERATOR DID
DURING THE POWER
FAILURE.

Now arrange the circled letters to form
the surprise answer, as suggested by the
above cartoon.

Print answer here ⬡⬡⬡⬡⬡ **ITS** ⬡⬡⬡⬡

JUMBLE

Unscramble these four Jumbles, one letter to
each square, to form four ordinary words.

RUSUY

YOULS

NOMOAR

UPGLEN

WON FIRST PRIZE
AT THE CAT SHOW.

Now arrange the circled letters to form
the surprise answer, as suggested by the
above cartoon.

*Print
answer* A
here

67

JUMBLE®

Unscramble these four Jumbles, one letter to
each square, to form four ordinary words.

TOYBO

KUYDS

GOAUNT

ZIRDAL

WHAT DID ONE
SKUNK SAY
TO THE OTHER?

Now arrange the circled letters to form
the surprise answer, as suggested by the
above cartoon.

Print answer here ◯◯ ◯◯ ◯◯◯ !

JUMBLE

Unscramble these four Jumbles, one letter to
each square, to form four ordinary words.

GRUPE

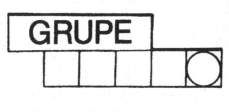

BLAYM

DYRAMI

OTTYNK

WHAT COMES INTO
A HOUSE THROUGH
THE KEYHOLE?

Now arrange the circled letters to form
the surprise answer, as suggested by the
above cartoon.

Print answer here

JUMBLE®

Unscramble these four Jumbles, one letter to
each square, to form four ordinary words.

MYRIG

ATHEW

DASSIT

POWNEA

Psst!

WHAT THE
SECRETIVE
MUMMIES KEPT.

Now arrange the circled letters to form
the surprise answer, as suggested by the
above cartoon.

Print
answer
here

◯◯◯◯◯◯ UNDER ◯◯◯◯◯

JUMBLE®

Unscramble these four Jumbles, one letter to each square, to form four ordinary words.

LIXEE

YINCC

TIPIDE

BAAMEO

HELPS CONSTRUCTION WORKERS TO STICK TOGETHER.

Now arrange the circled letters to form the surprise answer, as suggested by the above cartoon.

Print answer here

JUMBLE®

Unscramble these four Jumbles, one letter to each square, to form four ordinary words.

HINKT

ROLGY

ENDOTE

SABBOR

THE TEACHER HAD TO WEAR DARK GLASSES BECAUSE ALL THE KIDS WERE THIS.

Now arrange the circled letters to form the surprise answer, as suggested by the above cartoon.

Print answer here

JUMBLE®

Unscramble these four Jumbles, one letter to
each square, to form four ordinary words.

VOLEN
◯ ◯

GHILT
◯ ◯

EXVONC
◯

LUDSON
◯ ◯

WHAT SHE SENSED
VIOLETS MIGHT
"SIGNIFY."

Now arrange the circled letters to form
the surprise answer, as suggested by the
above cartoon.

Print answer here " ◯◯ ' ◯ ◯◯◯◯◯ "

JUMBLE®

Unscramble these four Jumbles, one letter to each square, to form four ordinary words.

LISEA

UNGED

LAWTUN

MORRAY

Doesn't surprise ME!

WHAT YOU MIGHT SAY WHEN YOU THINK OF A CHILD PRODIGY.

Now arrange the circled letters to form the surprise answer, as suggested by the above cartoon.

Print answer here

⃝⃝⃝⃝⃝ ⃝⃝⃝⃝⃝⃝ !

JUMBLE®

Unscramble these four Jumbles, one letter to each square, to form four ordinary words.

VELOH

OXPRY

BOGTLE

NAWDDE

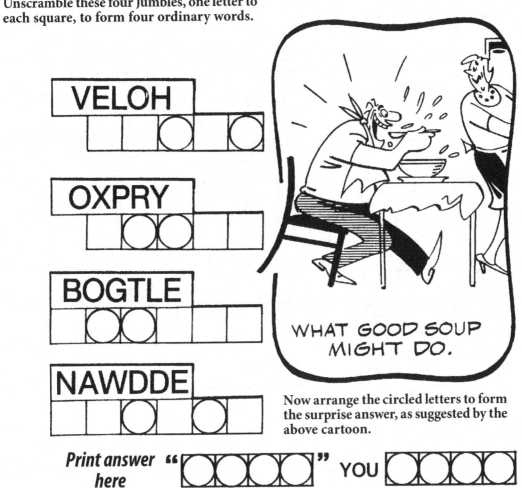

WHAT GOOD SOUP
MIGHT DO.

Now arrange the circled letters to form the surprise answer, as suggested by the above cartoon.

Print answer here " ◯◯◯◯◯ " YOU ◯◯◯◯

JUMBLE®

Unscramble these four Jumbles, one letter to
each square, to form four ordinary words.

NEWIT

BAWLY

BRUBRE

GELPED

WHAT YOU GET
PLENTIFULLY THESE
DAYS, WHEN YOU
DECIDE TO BUILD.

Now arrange the circled letters to form
the surprise answer, as suggested by the
above cartoon.

Print answer here

JUMBLE®

Unscramble these four Jumbles, one letter to
each square, to form four ordinary words.

RUYLB

TURTE

FUITTO

LOCCIA

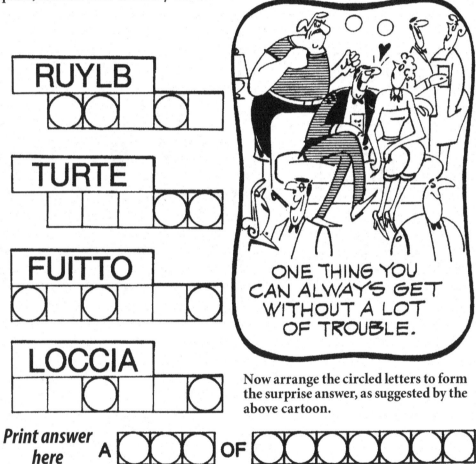

ONE THING YOU
CAN ALWAYS GET
WITHOUT A LOT
OF TROUBLE.

Now arrange the circled letters to form
the surprise answer, as suggested by the
above cartoon.

**Print answer
here** A ☐☐☐ OF ☐☐☐☐☐☐☐

JUMBLE®

Unscramble these four Jumbles, one letter to
each square, to form four ordinary words.

GATEA

WARLC

DOUXES

IMRAUD

FROM WHICH RICHES
HAVE BEEN KNOWN
TO COME.

Now arrange the circled letters to form
the surprise answer, as suggested by the
above cartoon.

Print answer here

JUMBLE

Unscramble these four Jumbles, one letter to each square, to form four ordinary words.

KYKIN

LAASI

FLOUWE

GRUHNY

Time for new blood

WHY THE VETERAN POLITICIAN DECIDED NOT TO RUN FOR OFFICE ANYMORE.

Now arrange the circled letters to form the surprise answer, as suggested by the above cartoon.

Print answer here   HE COULD ◯◯◯◯◯◯◯◯

JUMBLE®

Unscramble these four Jumbles, one letter to
each square, to form four ordinary words.

YUTIN

LAHZE

IKIBIN

YOHRFT

I made your favor-
ite dish, dear

WHAT TO DO IF YOUR
WIFE SOMETIMES
DOESN'T TREAT YOU
AS SHE SHOULD.

Now arrange the circled letters to form
the surprise answer, as suggested by the
above cartoon.

Print answer here

80

JUMBLE®

Unscramble these four Jumbles, one letter to
each square, to form four ordinary words.

AKQUE

TARIE

FLUWAL

INFFUM

YAK
YAK YAK

HE BOUGHT HIS
WIFE A MINK TO
KEEP HER THIS.

Now arrange the circled letters to form
the surprise answer, as suggested by the
above cartoon.

*Print answer
here*
 — &

JUMBLE®

Unscramble these four Jumbles, one letter to each square, to form four ordinary words.

TIVER

ESTAE

WAYYAN

PYRSOD

WHAT THE GUY WHO MADE A PASS AT THE WRONG GIRL GOT.

Now arrange the circled letters to form the surprise answer, as suggested by the above cartoon.

Print answer here INTO ◯◯◯◯◯ ◯◯◯◯◯◯

JUMBLE®

Unscramble these four Jumbles, one letter to each square, to form four ordinary words.

TENKO

MAIDT

YAXLAG

HERBAC

A DOCTOR WHO GIVES MEDICAL CARE WITH-OUT CHARGING MUST BE DOING THIS.

Now arrange the circled letters to form the surprise answer, as suggested by the above cartoon.

Print answer here "◯◯◯◯◯◯◯◯◯◯"

JUMBLE®

Unscramble these four Jumbles, one letter to each square, to form four ordinary words.

ELCEX

UGLID

RUNUTE

HEHRST

Hmmm—guess I can't pass for 29 any more

A WOMAN USUALLY STOPS TELLING HER AGE WHEN IT STARTS THIS.

Now arrange the circled letters to form the surprise answer, as suggested by the above cartoon.

Print answer here ☐☐☐☐☐☐☐ ON ☐☐☐

84

JUMBLE®

Unscramble these four Jumbles, one letter to
each square, to form four ordinary words.

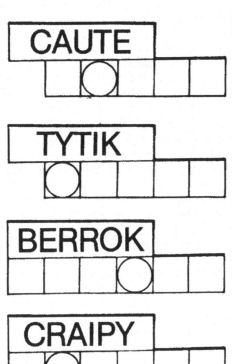

CAUTE

TYTIK

BERROK

CRAIPY

IF YOU DON'T HAVE
A LEG TO STAND
ON, IT'S BEST NOT
TO DO THIS.

Now arrange the circled letters to form
the surprise answer, as suggested by the
above cartoon.

Print answer here 〇〇〇〇

JUMBLE®

Unscramble these four Jumbles, one letter to
each square, to form four ordinary words.

BROIN

SIBAN

GERDED

DACAFE

Don't want to
get involved

HE STOPPED TAKING
HER OUT WHEN SHE
STARTED HAVING
THIS.

Now arrange the circled letters to form
the surprise answer, as suggested by the
above cartoon.

Print answer here " ◯◯◯◯◯ " ◯◯◯◯◯

JUMBLE®

Unscramble these four Jumbles, one letter to each square, to form four ordinary words.

ESROU

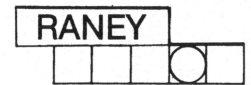

RANEY

COYPIL

NORGAD

EXPECTED TO GET
IN TOUCH WITH
A RECEIVER.

Now arrange the circled letters to form the surprise answer, as suggested by the above cartoon.

Print answer here

JUMBLE®

Unscramble these four Jumbles, one letter to
each square, to form four ordinary words.

SCOUF

LUVEA

NONITE

MEHRAM

WHAT THE GOSSIP
TURNED AN
EARFUL INTO.

Now arrange the circled letters to form
the surprise answer, as suggested by the
above cartoon.

Print answer here A ☐☐☐☐☐☐☐☐☐

88

JUMBLE®

Unscramble these four Jumbles, one letter to each square, to form four ordinary words.

GIBLE

NUKKS

HOCCUR

TEBICS

FOR A MOTHER, THE SON ALWAYS DOES THIS.

Now arrange the circled letters to form the surprise answer, as suggested by the above cartoon.

Print answer here

JUMBLE®

Unscramble these four Jumbles, one letter to
each square, to form four ordinary words.

DOFOL

JYKER

CLAJEO

MOUPID

Hurray—I landed him!

WHAT A SPINSTER
MIGHT DO DURING
LEAP YEAR.

Now arrange the circled letters to form
the surprise answer, as suggested by the
above cartoon.

Print answer here

JUMBLE®

Unscramble these four Jumbles, one letter to
each square, to form four ordinary words.

COINT

ROBAR

EKATIN

KRUNEB

TRAVEL

8TH
NATIONAL

EUROPE

SPAIN

AFRICA

ASIA

VISIT
SUNNY
ITALY

THE BEST BOOK
TO STUDY BEFORE
PLANNING A
BIG TRIP.

Now arrange the circled letters to form
the surprise answer, as suggested by the
above cartoon.

Print answer here THE ⬡⬡⬡⬡⬡⬡⬡⬡⬡

JUMBLE®

Unscramble these four Jumbles, one letter to
each square, to form four ordinary words.

UGIED

GYANT

JELDIA

VAHBEE

WHERE THAT POTTERY
THIEF WILL PROBABLY
END UP.

Now arrange the circled letters to form
the surprise answer, as suggested by the
above cartoon.

Print answer here

92

JUMBLE®

Unscramble these four Jumbles, one letter to
each square, to form four ordinary words.

VOARP
⬜⬜⭕⬜⬜⭕

GELEY
⬜⬜⭕⬜⭕

UMSCAP
⬜⬜⬜⭕⭕⬜

HEYBER
⭕⬜⬜⬜⬜⭕

WHAT MOST POETS
WILL TELL YOU.

Now arrange the circled letters to form
the surprise answer, as suggested by the
above cartoon.

Print answer
here
⭕⭕⭕⭕⭕⭕ DOESN'T ⭕⭕⭕

JUMBLE®

Unscramble these four Jumbles, one letter to
each square, to form four ordinary words.

LANVA

ZAMIE

RESEGY

MANIAE

No use. None of
them are eligible

A SINGLE GIRL LOOK-
ING FOR A HUSBAND
SHOULD LOOK FOR
THIS INSTEAD.

Now arrange the circled letters to form
the surprise answer, as suggested by the
above cartoon.

Print answer here A ⬡⬡⬡⬡⬡⬡⬡ ⬡⬡⬡

JUMBLE®

Unscramble these four Jumbles, one letter to
each square, to form four ordinary words.

TOXEL

BOUMG

ROOHRR

HALNIE

COULD BE CALLED
THE CENTER OF THE
REVOLUTION.

Now arrange the circled letters to form
the surprise answer, as suggested by the
above cartoon.

Print answer here ◯◯◯ ◯◯◯

JUMBLE®

Unscramble these four Jumbles, one letter to each square, to form four ordinary words.

NEALK

CLIVI

HOWALL

LOOSAN

He says he owes it all to that ____

A KIND OF STRENGTH TO BE FOUND IN WINES.

Now arrange the circled letters to form the surprise answer, as suggested by the above cartoon.

Print answer here "  "

JUMBLE

Unscramble these four Jumbles, one letter to
each square, to form four ordinary words.

PEALL

YITED

WYIHNN

BOULED

A GIRL CAN BE
PRETTY AS A
PICTURE WHEN
SHE'S THIS.

Now arrange the circled letters to form
the surprise answer, as suggested by the
above cartoon.

*Print
answer
here*

☐◯◯◯◯ — ◯◯◯◯◯◯◯◯◯

97

JUMBLE®

Unscramble these four Jumbles, one letter to each square, to form four ordinary words.

NAKOE

DUCIL

ORREBB

DACROW

A DRESS THAT MAKES YOU LOOK SLIM OFTEN MAKES OTHERS DO THIS.

Now arrange the circled letters to form the surprise answer, as suggested by the above cartoon.

Print answer here

JUMBLE®

Unscramble these four Jumbles, one letter to each square, to form four ordinary words.

HEMTY

LIENN

NAVIED

FEBRYL

THE BEST WAY TO
KEEP THIN IS NOT
TO EXCEED THIS:

Now arrange the circled letters to form the surprise answer, as suggested by the above cartoon.

Print answer here THE " ◯◯◯◯ " ◯◯◯◯◯

JUMBLE®

Unscramble these four Jumbles, one letter to each square, to form four ordinary words.

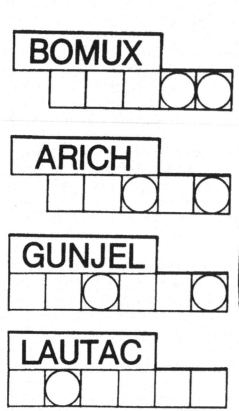

BOMUX

ARICH

GUNJEL

LAUTAC

Meet the guy I'm going to marry

That's what SHE thinks!

A LOVE AFFAIR THAT NATURALLY HAS A MAN IN THE MIDDLE OF IT.

Now arrange the circled letters to form the surprise answer, as suggested by the above cartoon.

Print answer here " ⬡⬡ - ⬡⬡⬡ - ⬡⬡ "

JUMBLE®

Unscramble these four Jumbles, one letter to
each square, to form four ordinary words.

ETHAL

CALVO

GAAMED

FALACI

WHAT'S YOUR SON
TAKING IN COLLEGE?

Now arrange the circled letters to form
the surprise answer, as suggested by the
above cartoon.

*Print
answer
here*

" ☐☐☐ ☐'☐☐ ☐☐☐ "

JUMBLE®

Unscramble these four Jumbles, one letter to
each square, to form four ordinary words.

PAPYL

NENAH

MUTTOS

KRUBEE

I'm exhausted

STAGE DOOR

HOW THE HULA
DANCER FELT AFTER
A HARD DAY'S
WORK.

Now arrange the circled letters to form
the surprise answer, as suggested by the
above cartoon.

Print answer here

JUMBLE®

Unscramble these four Jumbles, one letter to each square, to form four ordinary words.

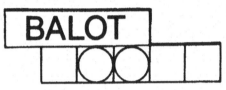

BALOT

TABEA

YOMPLE

GOURAC

I warned you about eating all that candy

DENTIST

IF IT ACHES, THERE COULD BE A MORAL TO BE "DRAWN."

Now arrange the circled letters to form the surprise answer, as suggested by the above cartoon.

Print answer here A " ⬡⬡⬡⬡⬡ "

JUMBLE®

Unscramble these four Jumbles, one letter to each square, to form four ordinary words.

WROCE

SHIWK

CUCHIP

ATTORE

WHAT THE SAFE-CRACKER TURNED COMEDIAN WAS.

Now arrange the circled letters to form the surprise answer, as suggested by the above cartoon.

Print answer here **A**

104

JUMBLE®

Unscramble these four Jumbles, one letter to each square, to form four ordinary words.

OPUCE

UFORR

DAPRON

SILAMY

IF YOU HAVE DOUBTS ABOUT WHETHER THE OLD PRINTING PRESS WORKS, ASK TO SEE THIS.

Now arrange the circled letters to form the surprise answer, as suggested by the above cartoon.

Print answer here ◯◯◯◯ " ◯◯◯◯◯ "

JUMBLE®

Unscramble these four Jumbles, one letter to
each square, to form four ordinary words.

KICCH

CAPEN

ZEEWEH

EEPPUK

WHAT A THIEF
MAY DO — AND SO
ARREST HIM!

Now arrange the circled letters to form
the surprise answer, as suggested by the
above cartoon.

Print answer here " ◯◯◯◯◯ "

JUMBLE®

Unscramble these four Jumbles, one letter to
each square, to form four ordinary words.

ONSOW
☐☐◯◯☐

BYASS
☐◯☐◯

CEXIES
☐☐☐☐◯☐

SINIST
☐◯◯☐◯☐

He sure went
up fast!

Doesn't
surprise ME!

VICE-
PRESID

IF AT FIRST YOU
DO SUCCEED, YOU'RE
PROBABLY THIS.

Now arrange the circled letters to form
the surprise answer, as suggested by the
above cartoon.

*Print answer
here*   THE ◯◯◯◯◯'◯ ◯◯◯

JUMBLE®

Unscramble these four Jumbles, one letter to
each square, to form four ordinary words.

NYVER

AGDEA

FADGYL

GLANJE

Let's go over
this again

REAL
ESTATE

BEFORE SIGNING THIS,
IT MIGHT BE READ
BACK ALSO.

Now arrange the circled letters to form
the surprise answer, as suggested by the
above cartoon.

Print answer here " ⃝⃝⃝⃝ "

108

JUMBLE®

Unscramble these four Jumbles, one letter to
each square, to form four ordinary words.

LAVIE

BABIR

INOUSC

YAWTER

IT TURNED INTO A
GAME OF THIS.

Now arrange the circled letters to form
the surprise answer, as suggested by the
above cartoon.

Print answer " ⬡⬡⬡⬡ ⬡⬡⬡⬡⬡ "
here

JUMBLE

Unscramble these four Jumbles, one letter to
each square, to form four ordinary words.

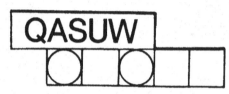

QASUW

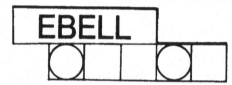

EBELL

BLUMJE

REYMOB

How about
—some heat?!

JANITOR

THEY COME UP
BOILING.

Now arrange the circled letters to form
the surprise answer, as suggested by the
above cartoon.

Print answer here

JUMBLE®

Unscramble these four Jumbles, one letter to
each square, to form four ordinary words.

FLAYE

POZAT

GLEEBA

SORIAL

Okay

WHAT A HUSBAND
USUALLY DOES WHEN
HE WANTS TO GET
IN THE LAST WORD.

Now arrange the circled letters to form
the surprise answer, as suggested by the
above cartoon.

Print answer here

JUMBLE®

Unscramble these four Jumbles, one letter to
each square, to form four ordinary words.

DURIL
☐ ◯◯ ☐

ANUFA
☐☐☐ ◯◯

KIALLA
☐☐☐☐ ◯ ☐

VORGEN
◯◯☐☐☐ ◯

WHAT A "PEDESTRIAN"
SORT OF PLAY IS
UNLIKELY TO HAVE.

Now arrange the circled letters to form
the surprise answer, as suggested by the
above cartoon.

Print answer here ◯ ◯◯◯◯ ◯◯◯

JUMBLE®

Unscramble these four Jumbles, one letter to
each square, to form four ordinary words.

NELIV

DARNB

NOBIAL

DELMAT

COMPLAIN ABOUT THE
TRAIN SERVICE.

Now arrange the circled letters to form
the surprise answer, as suggested by the
above cartoon.

Print answer here "◯◯◯◯"

113

JUMBLE®

Unscramble these four Jumbles, one letter to
each square, to form four ordinary words.

LITEE

IMMAX

MERCOH

PELSOG

MAY LEAD ONE
TO THE ALTAR.

Now arrange the circled letters to form
the surprise answer, as suggested by the
above cartoon.

Print answer here ◯◯◯ ◯◯◯◯◯

JUMBLE®

Unscramble these four Jumbles, one letter to
each square, to form four ordinary words.

VUREC

BYNAD

TEYQUI

MOLDEY

FAMOUS IN THE
WORLD OF MUSIC.

Now arrange the circled letters to form
the surprise answer, as suggested by the
above cartoon.

Print answer here " ⬡⬡⬡⬡⬡ "

JUMBLE®

Unscramble these four Jumbles, one letter to
each square, to form four ordinary words.

CHOAM
◯◯ ◯

NICEW
◯ ◯ ◯

BERKAM
◯

NORREC
◯◯◯

FICTION

LATEST LOVE STORIES

WHAT ONE MIGHT
BE LOOKING FOR AT
THE LIBRARY.

Now arrange the circled letters to form
the surprise answer, as suggested by the
above cartoon.

Print
answer A ◯◯◯ ◯◯◯◯◯◯◯◯
here

JUMBLE®

Unscramble these four Jumbles, one letter to
each square, to form four ordinary words.

DENEY

GIBEE

WEGNIT

MERRIP

COULD BE EATING
— WITH A GREAT
DEAL OF NOISE.

Now arrange the circled letters to form
the surprise answer, as suggested by the
above cartoon.

Print answer here " ◯◯◯ – ◯◯◯ "

JUMBLE

Unscramble these four Jumbles, one letter to each square, to form four ordinary words.

POCUR
⬜⭕⭕⭕⬜

NIGIC
⬜⭕⭕⭕⬜

BINLEB
⬜⭕⬜⭕⬜⬜

WOLTAL
⭕⭕⬜⭕⬜⬜

CAN HELP TO AVOID FRICTION.

Now arrange the circled letters to form the surprise answer, as suggested by the above cartoon.

Print answer here
⭕⭕⭕⭕⭕⭕⭕⭕⭕⭕⭕⭕⭕

JUMBLE®

Unscramble these four Jumbles, one letter to each square, to form four ordinary words.

YORAF

LAQUI

PLUXED

TOBENN

MAY GO AROUND HUMMING.

Now arrange the circled letters to form the surprise answer, as suggested by the above cartoon.

Print answer here

JUMBLE®

Unscramble these four Jumbles, one letter to each square, to form four ordinary words.

CAUMS

LAGOW

KLUNIE

REELCY

Almost
overslept

Gonna get high-
paying jobs

HELPS MANY
PEOPLE RISE IN
THE WORLD.

Now arrange the circled letters to form the surprise answer, as suggested by the above cartoon.

Print answer here AN ◯◯◯◯◯◯ ◯◯◯◯◯◯

JUMBLE®

Unscramble these four Jumbles, one letter to each square, to form four ordinary words.

NILOG

TYFFA

SLABAM

PARMEC

POINTED IN ONE
DIRECTION AND
HEADED IN THE
OTHER.

Now arrange the circled letters to form the surprise answer, as suggested by the above cartoon.

Print answer here

121

JUMBLE®

Unscramble these four Jumbles, one letter to
each square, to form four ordinary words.

ORSAL

SHAQU

MEEZAC

ZELZUG

DO something about it!

TOO MANY OF
THESE CAN MAKE
A PERSON LOOK
ROUND.

Now arrange the circled letters to form
the surprise answer, as suggested by the
above cartoon.

*Print
answer
here*   "⬡⬡⬡⬡⬡⬡" ⬡⬡⬡⬡⬡

JUMBLE®

Unscramble these four Jumbles, one letter to each square, to form four ordinary words.

MEFAD

WILLT

BLAGOM

FLARTE

Where is he?

WHAT THE COOK DID AFTER HE CRACKED AN EGG.

Now arrange the circled letters to form the surprise answer, as suggested by the above cartoon.

Print answer here

JUMBLE®

Unscramble these four Jumbles, one letter to
each square, to form four ordinary words.

EUQUE

YANDS

BOPHIS

MIRADS

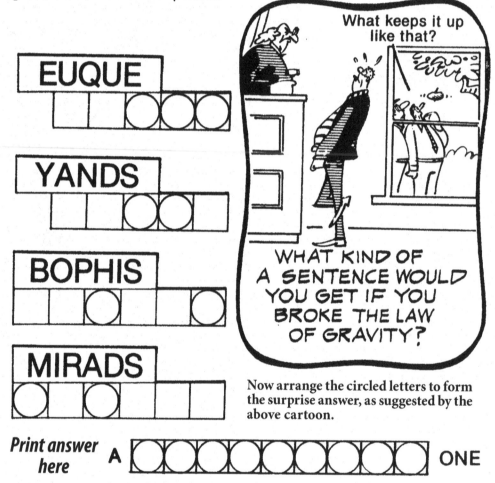

What keeps it up
like that?

WHAT KIND OF
A SENTENCE WOULD
YOU GET IF YOU
BROKE THE LAW
OF GRAVITY?

Now arrange the circled letters to form
the surprise answer, as suggested by the
above cartoon.

**Print answer
here** A ◯◯◯◯◯◯◯◯◯◯◯ **ONE**

JUMBLE®

Unscramble these four Jumbles, one letter to each square, to form four ordinary words.

DUWNE

ULLKS

FOYFAP

GRUFIE

HOW DID THE PIG GET ACROSS THE OCEAN?

Now arrange the circled letters to form the surprise answer, as suggested by the above cartoon.

Print answer here THE ◯◯◯◯◯ "◯◯◯"

JUMBLE®

Unscramble these four Jumbles, one letter to
each square, to form four ordinary words.

WHISS

LOOGI

GRAHAN

HERTIE

WHAT THE GUARD
AT THE HAUNTED
HOUSE SAID.

Now arrange the circled letters to form
the surprise answer, as suggested by the
above cartoon.

**Print answer
here** ◯◯◯ ◯◯◯◯◯ THERE **?**

126

JUMBLE®

Unscramble these four Jumbles, one letter to each square, to form four ordinary words.

KERCE

DOUMI

JICTEN

REGOFT

WHAT THE MOUSE SAID WHEN HIS TAIL GOT CAUGHT IN THE TRAP.

Now arrange the circled letters to form the surprise answer, as suggested by the above cartoon.

Print answer here THAT'S THE ⬡⬡⬡ OF ⬡⬡ !

JUMBLE®

Unscramble these four Jumbles, one letter to
each square, to form four ordinary words.

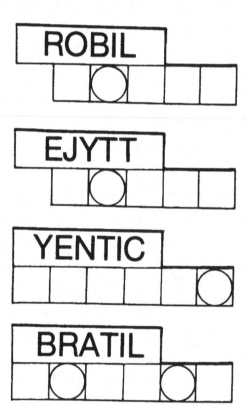

ROBIL

EJYTT

YENTIC

BRATIL

Fasten seat belts,
we're arriving

STOCKS

MIGHT DESCRIBE THE
FEELING YOU SOMETIMES
GET WHEN A PLANE
DESCENDS.

Now arrange the circled letters to form
the surprise answer, as suggested by the
above cartoon.

Print answer here " ◯◯◯ – ◯◯ "

JUMBLE®

Unscramble these four Jumbles, one letter to
each square, to form four ordinary words.

ROBEW

DARTY

FLIXUN

GORCED

WHAT THE TAILOR
CALLED HIS
PARTNER.

Now arrange the circled letters to form
the surprise answer, as suggested by the
above cartoon.

**Print answer
here** HIS "⬡⬡⬡⬡⬡⬡" ⬡⬡⬡

JUMBLE®

Unscramble these four Jumbles, one letter to each square, to form four ordinary words.

BLONE

KADEB

FRUTOH

PIGNUM

WHAT KNOCKING A BALL THROUGH A WINDOW MIGHT BE.

Now arrange the circled letters to form the surprise answer, as suggested by the above cartoon.

Print answer here " ☐☐☐☐☐☐☐ "

JUMBLE®

Unscramble these four Jumbles, one letter to each square, to form four ordinary words.

FINEK

KALCH

TENCCA

SHUBLE

TELLER

Sorry

WHAT YOU'D EXPECT PEOPLE WITH NO MONEY IN THE BANK TO WRITE.

Now arrange the circled letters to form the surprise answer, as suggested by the above cartoon.

Print answer here

PUZZLE
130

JUMBLE®

Unscramble these four Jumbles, one letter to each square, to form four ordinary words.

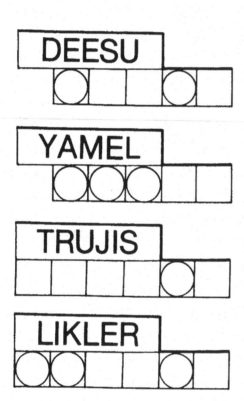

DEESU

YAMEL

TRUJIS

LIKLER

NUMISMATISTS' CONVENTION

WHAT THOSE COIN COLLECTORS ALWAYS GOT TOGETHER FOR.

Now arrange the circled letters to form the surprise answer, as suggested by the above cartoon.

Print answer here OLD ○○○○○ ' ○○○○

JUMBLE®

Unscramble these four Jumbles, one letter to
each square, to form four ordinary words.

PEXLE

VEREF

RUBBUS

SHAGAT

THE NEWSPAPERMAN
TURNED DRYCLEANER
BECAUSE HE DIDN'T
BELIEVE IN THIS.

Now arrange the circled letters to form
the surprise answer, as suggested by the
above cartoon.

Print answer here A ◯◯◯◯ " ◯◯◯◯◯ "

133

JUMBLE®

Unscramble these four Jumbles, one letter to
each square, to form four ordinary words.

YONOL

RAPPE

RETHOM

GLANID

Began
with
nothing

Next

A DOCTOR WHO
SPECIALIZES IN THIS
OFTEN STARTS
FROM SCRATCH.

Now arrange the circled letters to form
the surprise answer, as suggested by the
above cartoon.

Print answer here

JUMBLE

Unscramble these four Jumbles, one letter to
each square, to form four ordinary words.

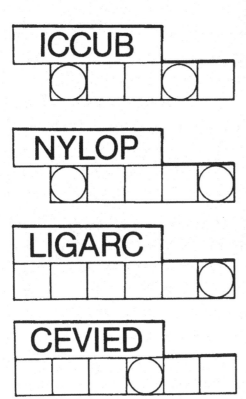

ICCUB

NYLOP

LIGARC

CEVIED

How
about
it?

CERTAINLY AN
OCCASION FOR
EATING OUT.

Now arrange the circled letters to form
the surprise answer, as suggested by the
above cartoon.

Print answer here A

135

JUMBLE®

Unscramble these four Jumbles, one letter to
each square, to form four ordinary words.

CRATT

DEHIC

MALBEC

TOEGEA

He's always
been a
finicky eater

THE FISH REFUSED TO
EAT THE WORM ON
THE HOOK BECAUSE HE
WAS AFRAID THERE
MIGHT BE THIS.

Now arrange the circled letters to form
the surprise answer, as suggested by the
above cartoon.

Print answer here A ⬡⬡⬡⬡⬡ ⬡⬡ IT

136

JUMBLE®

Unscramble these four Jumbles, one letter to each square, to form four ordinary words.

NOROH

FEBOG

ENGOUL

RAUBUE

Can't keep up with 'em anymore

THE FELLOW WHO USED TO RACE CARS QUIT BECAUSE HE COULD NO LONGER DO THIS.

Now arrange the circled letters to form the surprise answer, as suggested by the above cartoon.

Print answer here  FAST

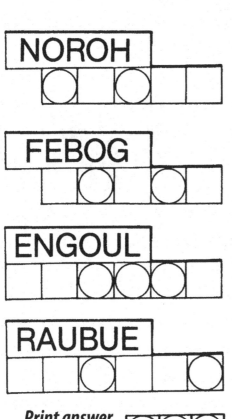

JUMBLE®

Unscramble these four Jumbles, one letter to
each square, to form four ordinary words.

WENOM

INJOT

DAGOIA

DOUBIT

Enjoy the
mountains

WHAT SOME HUSBANDS
WOULD LIKE TO DO
WHEN THEIR WIVES GO
TO THE COUNTRY.

Now arrange the circled letters to form
the surprise answer, as suggested by the
above cartoon.

Print answer here " ☐☐ ☐☐ ☐☐☐☐ "

JUMBLE

Unscramble these four Jumbles, one letter to each square, to form four ordinary words.

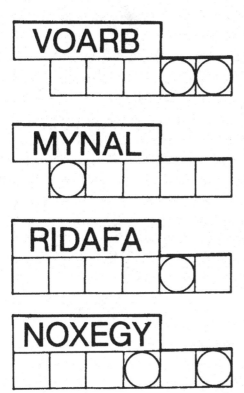

VOARB

MYNAL

RIDAFA

NOXEGY

WHAT KIND OF EXPERIENCE MIGHT IT BE WHEN YOU GAMBLE AWAY THE RENT MONEY?

Now arrange the circled letters to form the surprise answer, as suggested by the above cartoon.

Print answer here A "◯◯◯◯◯◯" ONE

JUMBLE®

Unscramble these four Jumbles, one letter to
each square, to form four ordinary words.

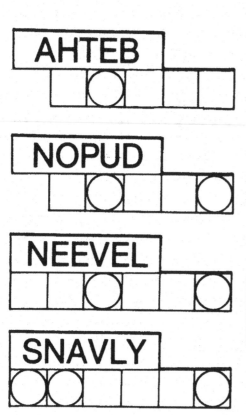

AHTEB

NOPUD

NEEVEL

SNAVLY

WHAT HE SAID WHEN
THE PSYCHIATRIST
ASKED WHETHER HE
HAD TROUBLE MAKING
UP HIS MIND.

Now arrange the circled letters to form
the surprise answer, as suggested by the
above cartoon.

Print answer here " ◯◯◯ ◯◯◯ ◯◯ "

140

JUMBLE®

Unscramble these four Jumbles, one letter to each square, to form four ordinary words.

PHARY

BOJAN

STAPOL

KOOCIE

THEY KEPT CALLING HIM A CRACKPOT UNTIL HE HIT THIS.

Now arrange the circled letters to form the surprise answer, as suggested by the above cartoon.

Print answer here THE ◯◯◯◯◯◯◯◯

141

JUMBLE®

Unscramble these four Jumbles, one letter to
each square, to form four ordinary words.

DREEL

VERPO

UNCLOM

SCOFIA

THUD!

HOW TO KEEP
FROM FALLING
OUT OF BED.

Now arrange the circled letters to form
the surprise answer, as suggested by the
above cartoon.

Print
answer
here

⬡⬡⬡⬡⬡ ON THE ⬡⬡⬡⬡⬡

JUMBLE®

Unscramble these four Jumbles, one letter to
each square, to form four ordinary words.

VANIE
◯◯◯◯◯

ARBSS
◯◯◯◯◯

GEBBUD
◯◯◯◯◯◯

GLEFUN
◯◯◯◯◯◯

WHAT THAT NUT
DECIDED TO GIVE UP
AFTER READING
ABOUT THE BAD
EFFECTS OF ALCOHOL.

Now arrange the circled letters to form
the surprise answer, as suggested by the
above cartoon.

Print answer here ◯◯◯◯◯◯◯◯

143

JUMBLE®

Unscramble these four Jumbles, one letter to
each square, to form four ordinary words.

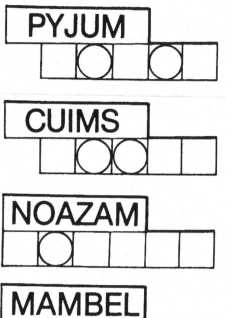

PYJUM

CUIMS

NOAZAM

MAMBEL

WHAT THE INSURANCE
COMPANY PAID
HIM WHEN HE
BUMPED HIS HEAD.

Now arrange the circled letters to form
the surprise answer, as suggested by the
above cartoon.

Print answer here A

JUMBLE ®

Unscramble these four Jumbles, one letter to each square, to form four ordinary words.

CHITK

HEWIG

THIECC

YAWMID

Double double toil and trouble

WHAT MACBETH WONDERED WHEN HE ENCOUNTERED THE THREE WEIRD SISTERS.

Now arrange the circled letters to form the surprise answer, as suggested by the above cartoon.

Print answer here

☐☐☐☐☐ WAS ☐☐☐☐☐

JUMBLE®

Unscramble these four Jumbles, one letter to
each square, to form four ordinary words.

IDLAY

INGYL

JERIGG

TYPAIR

YOU WOULDN'T CALL
THAT PRETTY
STEWARDESS THIS,
WOULD YOU?

Now arrange the circled letters to form
the surprise answer, as suggested by the
above cartoon.

Print answer
here   A "◯◯◯◯◯" ◯◯◯◯

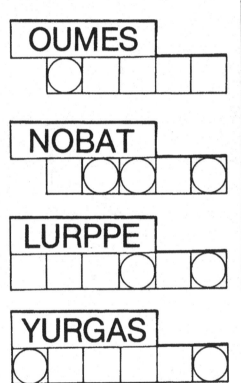

JUMBLE®

Unscramble these four Jumbles, one letter to each square, to form four ordinary words.

OUMES

NOBAT

LURPPE

YURGAS

THERE'S THAT ONE FEATURE ABOUT HIS NEW CAR THAT'S GUARANTEED TO LAST A LIFETIME.

Now arrange the circled letters to form the surprise answer, as suggested by the above cartoon.

Print answer here THE ⭕⭕⭕⭕⭕⭕⭕⭕⭕

147

JUMBLE®

Unscramble these four Jumbles, one letter to
each square, to form four ordinary words.

CADYE

FREGI

MIRVEN

PICTES

WHAT THE WHEELMAN
OF THE GETAWAY
CAR WAS.

Now arrange the circled letters to form
the surprise answer, as suggested by the
above cartoon.

Print
answer
here

A " ⭕⭕⭕⭕⭕ " ⭕⭕⭕⭕⭕⭕⭕

JUMBLE®

Unscramble these four Jumbles, one letter to
each square, to form four ordinary words.

RESEA
◯◯

YAHIR
◯ ◯

VOALAW
◯

SOWDAH
◯ ◯

WHY SHE CRITICIZED
HIM FOR STARTING
OFF ON THE
WRONG FOOT.

Now arrange the circled letters to form
the surprise answer, as suggested by the
above cartoon.

Print answer here IT ◯◯◯ ◯◯◯◯

JUMBLE®

Unscramble these four Jumbles, one letter to
each square, to form four ordinary words.

SOOME

CLATH

TALFOA

RILIXE

She sure LOOKS young

How does she manage it?

HOW SHE KEEPS HER AGE.

Now arrange the circled letters to form
the surprise answer, as suggested by the
above cartoon.

Print answer here ⬡⬡ ⬡⬡⬡⬡⬡⬡⬡

150

JUMBLE®

Unscramble these four Jumbles, one letter to each square, to form four ordinary words.

NAGIT

PHRAC

CEDITE

EGWAIH

SECOND HAND DEPT. MINUTE HAND DEPT. HOUR HAND DEPT.

WHAT YOU MIGHT EXPECT THE BOSS AT THE WATCH FACTORY TO DO WHEN THE WORKERS KEEP GOOFING OFF.

Now arrange the circled letters to form the surprise answer, as suggested by the above cartoon.

Print answer here

JUMBLE®

Unscramble these four Jumbles, one letter to
each square, to form four ordinary words.

TOOPH

LEROD

ISSUME

ABNOME

PSYCHIATRISTS DON'T
HAVE TO WORRY AS
LONG AS THIS
HAPPENS.

Now arrange the circled letters to form
the surprise answer, as suggested by the
above cartoon.

Print answer here

JUMBLE®

Unscramble these four Jumbles, one letter to
each square, to form four ordinary words.

UPOHC

WAKTE

YIMTID

GANNIA

Let's go out and disco!

WHAT HAPPENED
TO HIS GET—
UP-AND-GO?

Now arrange the circled letters to form
the surprise answer, as suggested by the
above cartoon.

Print answer here IT ⬡⬡⬡ ⬡⬡ & ⬡⬡⬡⬡

JUMBLE®

Unscramble these four Jumbles, one letter to
each square, to form four ordinary words.

PLUIT

TUFIR

EIVIDD

BYSTUL

WHAT THEIR NEIGHBOR
EXCHANGED FOR A
LITTLE SUGAR.

Now arrange the circled letters to form
the surprise answer, as suggested by the
above cartoon.

Print
answer
here
A ◯◯◯◯◯◯◯ "◯◯◯◯"

PUZZLE
153

JUMBLE®

Unscramble these four Jumbles, one letter to
each square, to form four ordinary words.

KRAAP

SESMY

SWUNIE

DAHNED

AJAX CO.
INVEST-
MENTS

HE SAID THAT
EVERY TIME HE SAW
HIS BROKER—

Now arrange the circled letters to form
the surprise answer, as suggested by the
above cartoon.

Print answer here ◯◯ ◯◯◯

155

JUMBLE®

Unscramble these four Jumbles, one letter to
each square, to form four ordinary words.

ANIFT

CHAPT

RASTIE

WISDON

WHAT THEY USUALLY ASK
FOR WHEN YOU HAVE
EVERY INTENTION OF
PAYING YOUR INCOME
TAX WITH A SMILE.

Now arrange the circled letters to form
the surprise answer, as suggested by the
above cartoon.

*Print answer
here*

JUMBLE®

Unscramble these four Jumbles, one letter to each square, to form four ordinary words.

YUSHK

CONTH

DYSTUR

DIVERF

WHEN TRYING TO LOSE WEIGHT, THIS IS THE THING TO AVOID FIRST.

Now arrange the circled letters to form the surprise answer, as suggested by the above cartoon.

Print answer here

157

JUMBLE®

Unscramble these four Jumbles, one letter to
each square, to form four ordinary words.

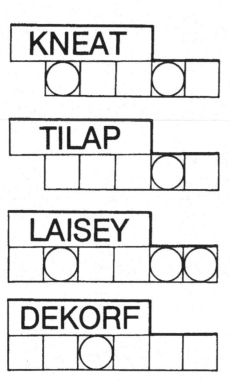

KNEAT

TILAP

LAISEY

DEKORF

REAL ESTATE

BANK

VERY "EASY" MORTGAGES

WHAT YOU MUST LEARN
ABOUT FIRST IF YOU
INTEND TO INVEST
IN REALTY.

Now arrange the circled letters to form
the surprise answer, as suggested by the
above cartoon.

Print answer here

158

JUMBLE®

Unscramble these four Jumbles, one letter to each square, to form four ordinary words.

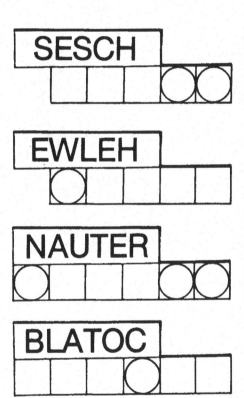

SESCH

EWLEH

NAUTER

BLATOC

WHAT A POLITICIAN WHO CLAIMS HE UNDER-STANDS ALL THE QUES-TIONS OF THE DAY USUALLY DOESN'T KNOW.

Now arrange the circled letters to form the surprise answer, as suggested by the above cartoon.

Print answer here THE ⬡⬡⬡⬡⬡⬡⬡

JUMBLE®

Unscramble these four Jumbles, one letter to
each square, to form four ordinary words.

YAGIL

MEERB

CUBDAT

DEBALE

WHAT HE DID THE
DAY HIS WIFE
GAVE BIRTH.

Now arrange the circled letters to form
the surprise answer, as suggested by the
above cartoon.

*Print answer
here*   ⬡⬡⬡⬡⬡ LIKE A ⬡⬡⬡⬡

JUMBLE®

Unscramble these four Jumbles, one letter to each square, to form four ordinary words.

HUMOT

TEQUS

SMIFLY

BONGLE

WHAT HE SAID AS HE WAS ABOUT TO LEAVE FOR WORK.

Now arrange the circled letters to form the surprise answer, as suggested by the above cartoon.

Print answer here ☐☐☐☐ FOR THE " ☐☐☐☐ "

JUMBLE®

Unscramble these four Jumbles, one letter to
each square, to form four ordinary words.

AZERC

DAPIL

TOALZE

LUFFIT

WHAT THAT PICNIC
TURNED INTO WHEN
IT BEGAN TO
DRIZZLE.

Now arrange the circled letters to form
the surprise answer, as suggested by the
above cartoon.

Print answer here A

162

JUMBLE

MAGIC

Challenger Puzzles

JUMBLE®

Unscramble these six Jumbles, one letter to
each square, to form six ordinary words.

DUPLED

CLUBEK

TINISS

REUMED

EECCAD

INGOPE

WHAT DAVID DID
TO GOLIATH.

Now arrange the circled letters to form
the surprise answer, as suggested by
the above cartoon.

Print answer here

" ◯◯◯◯◯◯◯ " HIM TO ◯◯◯◯◯

JUMBLE®

Unscramble these six Jumbles, one letter to each square, to form six ordinary words.

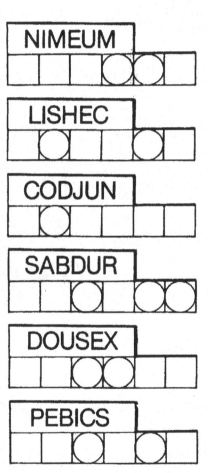

NIMEUM

LISHEC

CODJUN

SABDUR

DOUSEX

PEBICS

HOW THOSE SINGERS COMMUNICATED.

Now arrange the circled letters to form the surprise answer, as suggested by the above cartoon.

Print answer here

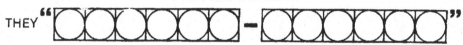

THEY " ⬡⬡⬡⬡⬡⬡⬡ — ⬡⬡⬡⬡⬡⬡ "

JUMBLE®

Unscramble these six Jumbles, one letter to each square, to form six ordinary words.

REBOFE

ASHIMP

BAUSCA

CHUGAT

FUNMIF

WEVILS

WHAT YOU SAW WHEN THOSE NEW NEXT-DOOR NEIGHBORS GAVE THEIR FIRST BIG PARTY.

Now arrange the circled letters to form the surprise answer, as suggested by the above cartoon.

Print answer here

THE ⬡⬡⬡⬡⬡ ⬡⬡⬡⬡⬡⬡⬡⬡

166

JUMBLE®

Unscramble these six Jumbles, one letter to each square, to form six ordinary words.

THORPY

PARAPE

MOINCE

PERREF

REGLED

CASMIO

WHERE THE LUMBERJACK WENT BEFORE CHRISTMAS.

Now arrange the circled letters to form the surprise answer, as suggested by the above cartoon.

Print answer here

ON " ⬚⬚⬚⬚⬚⬚⬚⬚⬚ " ⬚⬚⬚⬚⬚
A

JUMBLE®

Unscramble these six Jumbles, one letter to
each square, to form six ordinary words.

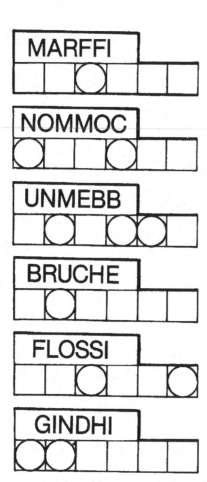

MARFFI

NOMMOC

UNMEBB

BRUCHE

FLOSSI

GINDHI

A very lonely man

WHAT THE
MISER KEPT.

Now arrange the circled letters to form
the surprise answer, as suggested by
the above cartoon.

Print answer here

TOO ⬡⬡⬡⬡⬡ TO ⬡⬡⬡⬡⬡⬡⬡⬡⬡

JUMBLE®

Unscramble these six Jumbles, one letter to each square, to form six ordinary words.

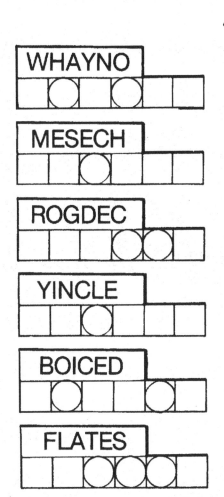

WHAYNO

MESECH

ROGDEC

YINCLE

BOICED

FLATES

IS THAT "SPOOK" WHO'S RUNNING FOR OFFICE LIKELY TO GET ELECTED?

Now arrange the circled letters to form the surprise answer, as suggested by the above cartoon.

Print answer here

NOT A ⬭⬭⬭⬭⬭ OF A ⬭⬭⬭⬭⬭⬭

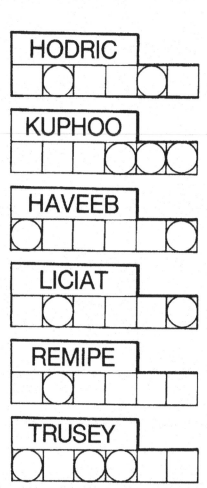

JUMBLE®

Unscramble these six Jumbles, one letter to each square, to form six ordinary words.

HODRIC

KUPHOO

HAVEEB

LICIAT

REMIPE

TRUSEY

DOWN WITH

BAN THE BO

WHAT A
TAILGATER IS.

Now arrange the circled letters to form the surprise answer, as suggested by the above cartoon.

Print answer here

A ⬡⬡⬡⬡⬡⬡⬡ ⬡⬡⬡⬡⬡⬡⬡⬡

JUMBLE

Unscramble these six Jumbles, one letter to
each square, to form six ordinary words.

REDONP

STYLUB

PANOWE

ASTUNE

KORREB

BUTSOE

At least THIS
is relaxing!

WHAT A MAN MIGHT
TRY TO DO ON
THE GOLF COURSE.

Now arrange the circled letters to form
the surprise answer, as suggested by
the above cartoon.

Print answer here

" ☐☐☐☐ " AWAY
HIS ☐☐☐☐☐☐☐☐☐

JUMBLE®

Unscramble these six Jumbles, one letter to each square, to form six ordinary words.

GIMINT

HUCNAH

PRYNTA

YOGAVE

CALDIP

CONTOY

Well! Glad to see you at work for a change!

WHAT THE CARTOGRAPHER WAS.

Now arrange the circled letters to form the surprise answer, as suggested by the above cartoon.

Print answer here

JUMBLE®

Unscramble these six Jumbles, one letter to
each square, to form six ordinary words.

RECRON

KLARET

YONTUB

TUMPIE

UNCHAP

KUPPEE

AN USHERETTE
SHOULD KNOW
HOW TO DO THIS.

Now arrange the circled letters to form
the surprise answer, as suggested by
the above cartoon.

Print answer here

◯◯◯ A ◯◯◯ IN
HIS ◯◯◯◯◯

JUMBLE®

Unscramble these six Jumbles, one letter to
each square, to form six ordinary words.

CIRNUH

SWERKE

SVALIE

FILRAY

REYJES

TIPOCE

It's a bargain at $450,000

WHAT INFLATION
MEANS.

Now arrange the circled letters to form
the surprise answer, as suggested by
the above cartoon.

Print answer here

A ⬡⬡⬡⬡⬡⬡ IN ⬡⬡⬡⬡⬡⬡

JUMBLE®

Unscramble these six Jumbles, one letter to each square, to form six ordinary words.

MINDOO
◯◯◯◯◯

LOUTAW
◯◯◯◯◯◯

WINDAR
◯◯◯◯◯◯

FUSULE
◯◯◯◯◯◯

DIMYAD
◯◯◯◯◯◯

RAFFAY
◯◯◯◯◯◯

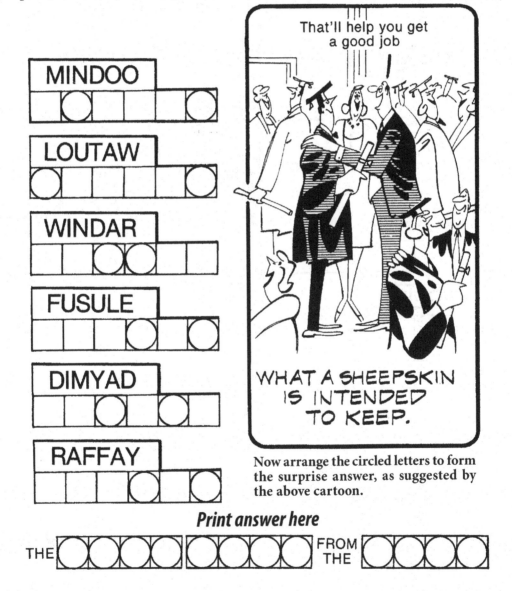

That'll help you get a good job

WHAT A SHEEPSKIN IS INTENDED TO KEEP.

Now arrange the circled letters to form the surprise answer, as suggested by the above cartoon.

Print answer here

THE ◯◯◯◯ ◯◯◯◯◯ FROM THE ◯◯◯◯

JUMBLE®

Unscramble these six Jumbles, one letter to
each square, to form six ordinary words.

METROH

PARTUB

HOTSUP

FREIHE

KATINE

STOLJE

How do you manage to
stay so slim?

IF YOU WANT
TO LOSE WEIGHT,
DON'T TALK ABOUT
IT—JUST DO THIS.

Now arrange the circled letters to form
the surprise answer, as suggested by
the above cartoon.

Print answer here

◯◯◯◯ YOUR ◯◯◯◯◯◯ ◯◯◯◯

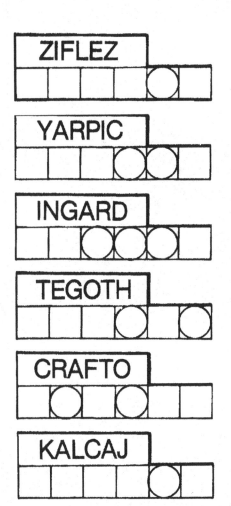

JUMBLE

Unscramble these six Jumbles, one letter to each square, to form six ordinary words.

ZIFLEZ

YARPIC

INGARD

TEGOTH

CRAFTO

KALCAJ

You may kiss the bride

WHEN THE BRIDE AND GROOM STARTED QUARRELING, IT MUST HAVE BEEN THIS.

Now arrange the circled letters to form the surprise answer, as suggested by the above cartoon.

Print answer here

AN " ☐☐☐☐☐ – ☐☐☐☐☐☐ "

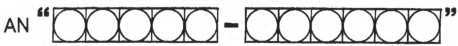

177

JUMBLE®

Unscramble these six Jumbles, one letter to
each square, to form six ordinary words.

MUHLIE

CUROGH

BELMAM

STANEF

ORDINO

JELGAN

WHAT A USED
CAR OFTEN IS.

Now arrange the circled letters to form
the surprise answer, as suggested by
the above cartoon.

Print answer here

◯◯◯ WHAT IT ◯◯◯◯◯ TO ◯◯

JUMBLE®

Unscramble these six Jumbles, one letter to each square, to form six ordinary words.

RUSHOC

GUIFER

DETUIL

FORTIP

SPOMIE

DESAUB

WHAT KIND
OF A GAME IS
FOOTBALL?

Now arrange the circled letters to form the surprise answer, as suggested by the above cartoon.

Print answer here

A ☐☐☐☐☐ & ☐☐☐☐☐☐ ONE

JUMBLE®

Unscramble these six Jumbles, one letter to each square, to form six ordinary words.

BEJARB

YALSAW

DIRNEH

TRAUGI

HADILA

VACIDE

How do you like my new designer outfit?

WHAT CLOTHES MAKE A WOMAN.

Now arrange the circled letters to form the surprise answer, as suggested by the above cartoon.

Print answer here

" ◯◯◯◯ " TO HER ◯◯◯◯◯◯◯

JUMBLE®

Unscramble these six Jumbles, one letter to each square, to form six ordinary words.

SAYMID

ANNOYE

GROAFE

BRUMPE

FLUINS

TYFARC

Must have had plenty of brains

But he wouldn't part with a penny

WHAT THAT CLEVER MISER WAS.

Now arrange the circled letters to form the surprise answer, as suggested by the above cartoon.

Print answer here

A ☐☐☐ OF ☐☐☐☐☐ ☐☐☐☐☐

JUMBLE®

Unscramble these six Jumbles, one letter to each square, to form six ordinary words.

RELENK

SEKTAG

FATOLA

MIBBIE

SMUCLY

CARPHE

Sniff

WHAT A GOOD WEATHERMAN IS SUPPOSED TO BE.

Now arrange the circled letters to form the surprise answer, as suggested by the above cartoon.

Print answer here

A " "

JUMBLE®

Unscramble these six Jumbles, one letter to each square, to form six ordinary words.

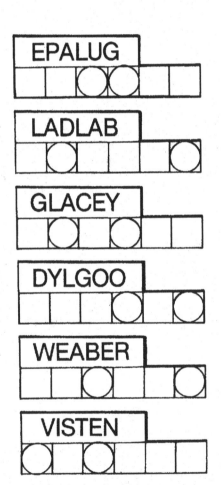

EPALUG

LADLAB

GLACEY

DYLGOO

WEABER

VISTEN

WHY THE HEIRS WERE NOT SURPRISED WHEN THE WILL WAS READ.

Now arrange the circled letters to form the surprise answer, as suggested by the above cartoon.

Print answer here

IT WAS A ☐☐☐☐☐ ☐☐☐☐☐☐☐☐☐

Answers

1. **Jumbles:** LILAC PAUSE JESTER KINGLY
   Answer: How she felt when she arrived home after a shopping binge—ALL "SPENT"

2. **Jumbles:** FORGO TEMPO CRAVAT LICHEN
   Answer: What kind of plans was the architect making for him?—TO GET HOME

3. **Jumbles:** BATON GLAND CRAYON HALVED
   Answer: What no upright person would do—LEAN

4. **Jumbles:** PRIOR MAUVE FORGET DULCET
   Answer: Words you might get from Voltaire—"I LOVE ART"

5. **Jumbles:** SUEDE GUESS CANOPY PALLID
   Answer: Did hangmen carry out such sentences?—SUSPENDED ONES

6. **Jumbles:** PEACE MANLY LIBIDO SYMBOL
   Answer: He couldn't remember—what this word meant—"AMNESIA"

7. **Jumbles:** EAGLE BRAVE MODISH NAUGHT
   Answer: What you might get from a debater—"BERATED"

8. **Jumbles:** LOONY ITCHY JUSTLY RADIAL
   Answer: How they bend their knees—"JOINT-LY"

9. **Jumbles:** YOUTH FORUM MISFIT ACCENT
   Answer: A job for someone who's well-padded—"CUSHY"

10. **Jumbles:** RAVEN VITAL EMERGE BICEPS
    Answer: A fruitful source of information—THE GRAPEVINE

11. **Jumbles:** PRONE VALVE FOURTH CAUCUS
    Answer: How they clapped their hands when she sang—OVER THEIR EARS

12. **Jumbles:** PRIZE LATCH OUTLET HARBOR
    Answer: What she hoped the bachelor would do about his way of life—"ALTAR" IT

13. **Jumbles:** EMBER PLAID NEGATE TANGLE
    Answer: What he had to do every time she had an accident in the kitchen—EAT IT FOR DINNER

14. **Jumbles:** TRACT PHOTO ENMITY SUBURB
    Answer: What a soap opera usually is—CORN ON THE SOB

15. **Jumbles:** DOILY ENSUE BEWARE COOKIE
    Answer: What the pretty blonde teacher was, as described by her pupils—BLUE-EYED

16. **Jumbles:** PARKA GRIEF CEMENT TRYING
    Answer: What's the best age to get hitched?—"MARRI-AGE"

17. **Jumbles:** PIANO FEINT DEBATE BEDBUG
    Answer: What a person who cheats on a diet is apt to do—GAIN—IN THE END

18. **Jumbles:** ANNUL JUMBO UNPACK PYTHON
    Answer: What an honest elevator man probably is—ON THE UP & UP

19. **Jumbles:** BLESS DIRTY FIRING INDOOR
    Answer: In this situation, you'll be very close to a fight—RINGSIDE

20. **Jumbles:** DECAY HOIST ASTRAY BAKERY
    Answer: Might be a current sensation—A SHOCK

21. **Jumbles:** GAUZE WALTZ NIMBLE GENIUS
    Answer: You need to bide your time to play this—THE WAITING GAME

22. **Jumbles:** EPOCH HAREM CASKET MOSQUE
    Answer: Made an impression on the bridle path—A HORSESHOE

23. **Jumbles:** DOWNY SORRY ELDEST PASTRY
    Answer: What a dictionary nut is never likely to be—AT A LOSS FOR WORDS

24. **Jumbles:** REBEL GAVEL STUDIO RABBIT
    Answer: What they said the dynamiters' annual shindig was—A REAL BLAST

25. **Jumbles:** GAUGE TACKY LIQUOR BEAVER
    Answer: No, he was not after the family pet—THE CAT BURGLAR

26. **Jumbles:** ELDER BRAWL QUORUM BUREAU
    Answer: Could make one think of food—a line of men waiting for haircuts—A "BARBER QUEUE" (barbecue)

27. **Jumbles:** BROIL WHEEL ENCORE OMELET
    Answer: What the newcomer made—"MEN COWER"

28. **Jumbles:** COUGH GIANT INLAND MINGLE
    Answer: This is the key to all good driving—IGNITION

29. **Jumbles:** AWARD OUNCE GOPHER INBORN
    Answer: Might provide some rest for a tired fish—THE OCEAN BED

30. **Jumbles:** WAFER RAINY STURDY CROTCH
    Answer: Due for a "roasting" from the sergeant—A "RAW" RECRUIT

31. **Jumbles:** FINAL AWOKE POSTAL BARREL
    Answer: Could be the result of spinning a lot of tales—A WEB OF LIES

32. **Jumbles:** FLOUR ALTAR NIPPLE CANINE
    Answer: For someone who plans to make a splash in the kitchen—AN APRON

33. **Jumbles:** BOWER FLANK GATHER FIDDLE
    Answer: Still a student—but he has within him the ability to make money—A "L-EARNER"

34. **Jumbles:** LADLE FUSSY DEPUTY CUDGEL
    Answer: How he looked after spending the whole day planting the garden—"SEEDY"

35. **Jumbles:** PIETY MOUTH NEWEST STRONG
    Answer: It's set to leave you in the dark—THE SUN (the sunset)

36. **Jumbles:** LYING ERASE BRIDLE CUDDLE
    Answer: Obviously not a fly-by-night—THE EARLY BIRD

37. **Jumbles:** PATIO STEED CENSUS BLAZER
    Answer: Suggested that he was proud of the fact that he worked less than anyone else—AN IDLE BOAST

38. **Jumbles:** CHESS FOYER TUMULT JUMPER
    Answer: To know this was the very apex of the spy's ambition—A TOP SECRET

39. **Jumbles:** BULLY LOWLY AFRAID ELEVEN
    Answer: The sort of life you might expect a glutton to lead—A FULL ONE

40. **Jumbles:** CATCH DAILY ABRUPT MEDLEY
    Answer: Where's the most difficult lock to pick?—ON A BALD HEAD

41. **Jumbles:** MUSTY PEONY ENGINE CRABBY
    Answer: A title the boxer didn't aim to be out for—"COUNT"

42. **Jumbles:** POISE TUNED SCHOOL KILLER
    Answer: When is a joke most effective?—WHEN IT STRIKES ONE

43. **Jumbles:** CRANK PLUSH EXCITE BOUNCE
    Answer: The "disintegration" of one star may threaten the whole nation—"TREASON"

44. **Jumbles:** SLANT COCOA WIDEST HERMIT
    Answer: Most duels are rather short affairs because they only require this—TWO SECONDS

45. **Jumbles:** FAVOR QUEEN AWHILE SATIRE
    Answer: Not a bad thing to do when in court—SWEAR

46. **Jumbles:** GRIME HAVEN ARTFUL ENOUGH
    Answer: What was the new bride's favorite fish?—"HER-RING"

47. **Jumbles:** CURIO FROZE ARCADE STOLEN
    Answer: What he had on as a result of getting into a pickle—A SOUR FACE

48. **Jumbles:** EMERY RAPID POLISH COMPEL
    Answer: How do you arrive at the top of a church steeple on a hot day?—"PER-SPIRE"

49. **Jumbles:** BORAX CAKED ABDUCT BUCKET
    Answer: What gardening that begins at daybreak often ends up with—"BACKBREAK"

50. **Jumbles:** RUSTY POACH JAGUAR INDUCE
    Answer: What people who cut you short on the phone evidently have—HANG-UPS

51. **Jumbles:** GLADE TRAIT MORGUE VACANT
    Answer: A GREAT OVEN might produce most of this—"OVEREATING"

52. **Jumbles:** EVOKE BUSHY DECADE LIKELY
    Answer: Vegetable that sound as though they should never be served aboard ships—LEEKS

53. **Jumbles:** DAUNT CROON INFECT FAULTY
    Answer: What some joggers tend to do—RUN TO FAT

54. **Jumbles:** GAILY FISHY KETTLE IMPAIR
    Answer: When they got married, this could have their "life's aim."—"FAMILIES"

55. **Jumbles:** ABOVE SNACK NUMBER INFUSE
    Answer: Could be the result of everyone wanting to get into the act—A MOB SCENE

56. **Jumbles:** DIZZY QUIRE WAITER URCHIN
    Answer: What a bright student is expected to do when there's an exam—WHIZ THROUGH THE QUIZ

57. **Jumbles:** GUILE ANNOY MORBID LAGOON
    Answer: This material never gets worn out—LINING

58. **Jumbles:** GUILT UNCLE ABOUND EYEFUL
    Answer: One is being pointlessly frank when speaking this way—BLUNTLY

59. **Jumbles:** BRIAR GOOSE AFFRAY DRUDGE
    Answer: A big wheel in the amusement business—FERRIS

60. **Jumbles:** FETCH NATAL PICNIC INDUCT
    Answer: Where you're apt to find the most fish—BETWEEN HEAD & TAIL

61. **Jumbles:** MINOR TWEET STIGMA CACTUS
    Answer: An easy way to get on TV—SIT ON YOUR SET

62. **Jumbles:** DRYLY OBESE SWIVEL DRIVEL
    Answer: What's a parrot?—A WORDY BIRDIE

63. **Jumbles:** TRIPE ROACH HYBRID TOTTER
    Answer: That THE RADIATOR produced—"A TORRID HEAT"

64. **Jumbles:** COLIC STOKE BLUING PRISON
    Answer: What the refrigerator did during the power failure—LOST ITS COOL

65. **Jumbles:** USURY LOUSY MAROON PLUNGE
    Answer: Won first prize at the cat show—A GLAMOUR PUSS

66. **Jumbles:** BOOTY DUSKY NOUGAT LIZARD
    Answer: What did one skunk say to the other?—SO DO YOU!

67. **Jumbles:** PURGE BALMY MYRIAD KNOTTY
    Answer: What comes into the house through the keyhole?—A KEY

68. **Jumbles:** GRIMY WHEAT SADIST WEAPON
    Answer: What the secretive mummies kept—THINGS UNDER WRAPS

69. **Jumbles:** EXILE CYNIC PITIED AMOEBA
    Answer: Helps construction workers to stick together—CEMENT

70. **Jumbles:** THINK GLORY DENOTE ABSORBS
    Answer: The teacher had to wear dark glasses because all the kids were this—SO BRIGHT

71. **Jumbles:** NOVEL LIGHT CONVEX UNSOLD
    Answer: What she sensed violets might "signify"—"IT'S LOVE"

72. **Jumbles:** AISLE NUDGE WALNUT ARMORY
    Answer: What you might say when you think of a child prodigy—SMALL WONDER

73. **Jumbles:** NOVEL PROXY GOBLET DAWNED
    Answer: What good soup might do—"BOWL" YOU OVER

74. **Jumbles:** TWINE BYLAW RUBBER PLEDGE
    Answer: What you get plentifully these days, when you decide to build—BILLED

75. **Jumbles:** BURLY UTTER OUTFIT CALICO
    Answer: One thing you can always get without a lot of trouble—A LOT OF TROUBLE

76. **Jumbles:** AGATE CRAWL EXODUS RADIUM
    Answer: From which riches have been known to come—RAGS

77. **Jumbles:** KINKY ALIAS WOEFUL HUNGRY
    Answer: Why the veteran politician decided not to run for office anymore—HE COULD ONLY WALK

78. **Jumbles:** UNITY HAZEL BIKINI FROTHY
    Answer: What to do if your wife sometimes doesn't treat you as she should—BE THANKFUL

79. **Jumbles:** QUAKE IRATE LAWFUL MUFFIN
    Answer: He bought his wife a mink to keep her this—WARM—& QUIET

80. **Jumbles:** RIVET TEASE ANYWAY DROPSY
    Answer: What the guy who made a pass at the wrong girl got—INTO DEEP WATER

81. **Jumbles:** TOKEN ADMIT GALAXY BREACH
    Answer: A doctor who gives medical care without charging must be this—"TREATING"

82. **Jumbles:** EXCEL GUILD UNTRUE THRESH
    Answer: A woman usually stops telling her age when it starts this—TELLING ON HER

83. **Jumbles:** ACUTE KITTY BROKER PIRACY
    Answer: If you don't have a leg to stand on, it's best not to do this—KICK

84. **Jumbles:** ROBIN BASIN DREDGE FACADE
    Answer: He stopped taking her out when she started having this—"BRIDE" IDEAS

85. **Jumbles:** ROUSE YEARN POLICY DRAGON
    Answer: Expected to get in touch with a receiver—YOUR EAR

86. **Jumbles:** FOCUS VALUE INTONE HAMMER
    Answer: What the gossip turned an earful into—A MOUTHFUL

87. **Jumbles:** BILGE SKUNK CROUCH BISECT
    Answer: For a mother, the son always does this—SHINES

88. **Jumbles:** FLOOD JERKY CAJOLE PODIUM
    Answer: What a spinster might do during leap year—JUMP FOR JOY

89. **Jumbles:** TONIC ARBOR INTAKE BUNKER
    Answer: The best book to study before planning a big trip—THE BANKBOOK

90. **Jumbles:** GUIDE TANGY JAILED BEHAVE
    Answer: Where that pottery thief will probably end up—IN THE JUG

91. **Jumbles:** VAPOR ELEGY CAMPUS HEREBY
    Answer: What most poets will tell you—RHYME DOESN'T PAY

92. **Jumbles:** NAVAL MAIZE GEYSER ANEMIA
    Answer: A single girl looking for a husband should look for this instead—A SINGLE MAN

93. **Jumbles:** EXTOL GUMBO HORROR INHALE
    Answer: Could be called the center of the revolution—THE HUB

94. **Jumbles:** ANKLE CIVIL HALLOW SALOON
    Answer: A kind of strength to be found in wines—"SINEW"

95. **Jumbles:** LAPEL DEITY WHINNY DOUBLE
    Answer: A girl can be pretty as a picture when she's this—WELL-PAINTED

96. **Jumbles:** OAKEN LUCID ROBBER COWARD
    Answer: A dress that makes you look slim often makes others do this—LOOK 'ROUND

97. **Jumbles:** THYME LINEN INVADE BELFRY
    Answer: The best way to keep thin is not to exceed this—THE "FEED" LIMIT

98. **Jumbles:** BUXOM CHAIR JUNGLE ACTUAL
    Answer: A love affair that naturally has a man in the middle of it—"RO-MAN-CE"

99. **Jumbles:** LATHE VOCAL DAMAGE FACIAL
    Answer: "What's your son taking in college?—"ALL I'VE GOT"

100. **Jumbles:** APPLY HENNA UTMOST REBUKE
    Answer: How the hula dancer felt after a hard day's work—SHAKY

101. **Jumbles:** BLOAT ABATE EMPLOY COUGAR
    Answer: If it aches, there could be a moral to be "drawn"—A "MOLAR"

102. **Jumbles:** COWER WHISK HICCUP ROTATE
    Answer: What the safecracker turned comedian was—A WISECRACKER

103. **Jumbles:** COUPE FUROR PARDON MISLAY
    Answer: If you have doubts about whether the old printing press works, ask to see this—SOME "PROOF"

104. **Jumbles:** CHICK PECAN WHEEZE UPKEEP
    Answer: What a thief may do—and so arrest him!—"PINCH"

105. **Jumbles:** SWOON ABYSS EXCISE INSIST
    Answer: If at first you DO succeed, you're probably this—THE BOSS'S SON

106. **Jumbles:** NERVY ADAGE GADFLY JANGLE
    Answer: Before signing this, it might be read back also—"DEED"

107. **Jumbles:** ALIVE RABBI COUSIN WATERY
    Answer: It turned into a game of this—"BASE BRAWL"

108. **Jumbles:** SQUAW BELLE JUMBLE EMBRYO
    Answer: They come up boiling—BUBBLES

109. **Jumbles:** LEAFY TOPAZ BEAGLE SAILOR
    Answer: What a husband usually does when he wants to get in the last word—APOLOGIZES

110. **Jumbles:** LURID FAUNA ALKALI GOVERN
    Answer: What a "pedestrian" sort of play is unlikely to have—A LONG RUN

111. **Jumbles:** LIVEN BRAND ALBINO MALTED
    Answer: Complain about the train service—"RAIL"

112. **Jumbles:** ELITE MAXIM CHROME GOSPEL
    Answer: May lead one to the altar—THE AISLE

113. **Jumbles:** CURVE BANDY EQUITY MELODY
    Answer: Famous in the world of music—"NOTED"

114. **Jumbles:** MOCHA WINCE EMBARK CORNER
    Answer: What one might be looking for at the library—A NEW ROMANCE

115. **Jumbles:** NEEDY BEIGE TWINGE PRIMER
    Answer: Could be eating—with a great deal of noise—"DIN-ING"

116. **Jumbles:** croup icing nibble tallow
    Answer: Can help to avoid friction—LUBRICATION

117. **Jumbles:** FORAY QUAIL DUPLEX BONNET
    Answer: May go around humming—A TOP

118. **Jumbles:** SUMAC AGLOW UNLIKE CELERY
    Answer: Helps many people rise in the world—AN ALARM CLOCK

119. **Jumbles:** LINGO TAFFY BALSAM CAMPER
    Answer: Pointed in one direction and headed in the other—A NAIL

120. **Jumbles:** SOLAR QUASH ECZEMA GUZZLE
    Answer: Too many of these can make a person look round—"SQUARE" MEALS

121. **Jumbles:** FAMED TWILL GAMBOL FALTER
    Answer: What the cook did after he cracked an egg—BEAT IT

122. **Jumbles:** QUEUE SANDY BISHOP DISARM
    Answer: What kind of a sentence would you get if you broke the law of gravity?—A SUSPENDED ONE

123. **Jumbles:** UNWED SKULL PAYOFF FIGURE
    Answer: How did the pig get across the ocean?—THE SWINE "FLU"

124. **Jumbles:** SWISH IGLOO HANGAR ETHER
    Answer: What the guard at the haunted house said—WHO GHOST THERE

125. **Jumbles:** CREEK ODIUM INJECT FORGET
    Answer: What the mouse said when his tail got caught in the trap—THAT'S THE END OF ME

126. **Jumbles:** BROIL JETTY NICETY TRIBAL
    Answer: Might describe the feeling you sometimes get when a plane descends—"EAR-RY"

127. **Jumbles:** BOWER TARDY INFLUX CODGER
    Answer: What the tailor called his partner—HIS "ALTER" EGO

128. **Jumbles:** NOBLE BAKED FOURTH IMPUGN
    Answer: What knocking a ball through a window might be—"PANEFUL"

129. **Jumbles:** KNIFE CHALK ACCENT BUSHEL
    Answer: What you'd expect people with no money in the bank to write—BLANK CHECKS

130. **Jumbles:** SUEDE MEALY JURIST KILLER
    Answer: What those coin collectors always got together for—OLD DIMES' SAKE

131. **Jumbles:** EXPEL FEVER SUBURB AGHAST
    Answer: The newspaperman turned dry cleaner because he didn't believe in this—A FREE "PRESS"

132. **Jumbles:** LOONY PAPER MOTHER LADING
    Answer: A doctor who specializes in this often starts from scratch--DERMATOLOGY

133. **Jumbles:** CUBIC PYLON GARLIC DEVICE
    Answer: Certainly an occasion for eating out—A PICNIC

134. **Jumbles:** TRACT CHIDE BECALM GOATEE
    Answer: The fish refused to eat the worm on the hook because he was afraid there might be this—A CATCH TO IT

135. **Jumbles:** HONOR BEFOG LOUNGE BUREAU
    Answer: The fellow who used to race cars quit because he could no longer do this—RUN FAST ENOUGH

136. **Jumbles:** WOMEN JOINT ADAGIO OUTBID
    Answer: What some husbands would like to do when their wives go to the country—"GO TO TOWN"

137. **Jumbles:** BRAVO MANLY AFRAID OXYGEN
    Answer: What kind of experience might it be when you gamble away the rent money?—A "MOVING" ONE

138. **Jumbles:** BATHE POUND ELEVEN SYLVAN
    Answer: What he said when the psychiatrist asked whether he had trouble making up his mine—"YES AND NO"

139. **Jumbles:** HARPY BANJO POSTAL COOKIE
Answer: They kept calling him a crackpot until he hit this—THE JACKPOT

140. **Jumbles:** ELDER PROVE COLUMN FIASCO
Answer: How to keep from falling out of bed—SLEEP ON THE FLOOR

141. **Jumbles:** NAIVE BRASS BEDBUG ENGULF
Answer: What that nut decided to give up after reading about the bad effects of alcohol—READING

142. **Jumbles:** JUMPY MUSIC AMAZON EMBALM
Answer: What the insurance company paid him when he bumped his head—A LUMP SUM

143. **Jumbles:** THICK WEIGH HECTIC MIDWAY
Answer: What Macbeth wondered when he encountered the three weird sisters—WHICH WAS WITCH

144. **Jumbles:** DAILY LYING JIGGER PARITY
Answer: You wouldn't call that pretty stewardess this, would you?—A "PLANE" GIRL

145. **Jumbles:** MOUSE BATON PURPLE SUGARY
Answer: There's that one feature about his new car that's guaranteed to last a lifetime—THE PAYMENTS

146. **Jumbles:** DECAY GRIEF VERMIN SEPTIC
Answer: What the wheelman of the getaway car was—A "SAFE" DRIVER

147. **Jumbles:** ERASE HAIRY AVOWAL SHADOW
Answer: Why she criticized him for starting off on the wrong foot—IT WAS HERS

148. **Jumbles:** MOOSE LATCH AFLOAT ELIXIR
Answer: How she keeps her age—TO HERSELF

149. **Jumbles:** GIANT PARCH DECEIT AWEIGH
Answer: What you might expect the boss at the watch factory to do when the workers keep goofing off—WATCH

150. **Jumbles:** PHOTO OLDER MISUSE BEMOAN
Answer: Psychiatrists don't have to worry as long as this happens—OTHERS DO

151. **Jumbles:** POUCH TWEAK DIMITY ANGINA
Answer: What happened to his get-up-and-go?—IT GOT UP & WENT

152. **Jumbles:** TULIP FRUIT DIVIDE SUBTLY
Answer: What their neighbor exchanged for a little sugar—A LITTLE "DIRT"

153. **Jumbles:** PARKA MESSY UNWISE HANDED
Answer: He said that every time he saw his broker—HE WAS

154. **Jumbles:** FAINT PATCH SATIRE DISOWN
Answer: What they usually ask for when you have every intention of paying your income tax with a smile—CASH INSTEAD

155. **Jumbles:** HUSKY NOTCH STURDY FERVID
Answer: When trying to lose weight, this is the thing to avoid first—SECONDS

156. **Jumbles:** TAKEN PLAIT EASILY FORKED
Answer: What you must learn about first if you intend to invest in realty--REALITY

157. **Jumbles:** CHESS WHEEL NATURE COBALT
Answer: What a politician who claims he understands all the questions of the day usually doesn't know—THE ANSWERS

158. **Jumbles:** GAILY EMBER ABDUCT BEADLE
Answer: What he did the day his wife gave birth—CRIED LIKE A BABY

159. **Jumbles:** MOUTH QUEST FLIMSY BELONG
Answer: What he said as he was about to leave for work—TIME FOR THE "BUSS"

160. **Jumbles:** CRAZE PLAID ZEALOT FITFUL
Answer: What that picnic turned into when it began to drizzle—A FIZZLE

161. **Jumbles:** PUDDLE BUCKLE INSIST DEMURE ACCEDE PIGEON
Answer: What David did to Goliath—"ROCKED" HIM TO SLEEP

162. **Jumbles:** IMMUNE CHISEL JOCUND ABSURD EXODUS BICEPS
Answer: How those singers communicated—THEY "CHORUS-PONDED"

163. **Jumbles:** BEFORE MISHAP ABACUS CAUGHT MUFFIN SWIVEL
Answer: What you saw when those new next-door neighbors gave their first big party—THE HOUSE SWARMING

164. **Jumbles:** TROPHY APPEAR INCOME PREFER LEDGER MOSAIC
Answer: Where the lumberjack went before Christmas—ON A "CHOPPING" SPREE

165. **Jumbles:** AFFIRM COMMON BENUMB CHERUB FOSSIL HIDING
Answer: What the miser kept—TOO MUCH TO HIMSELF

166. **Jumbles:** ANYHOW SCHEME CODGER NICELY BODICE FESTAL
Answer: Is that "spook" who's running for office likely to get elected?—NOT A GHOST OF A CHANCE

167. **Jumbles:** ORCHID HOOKUP BEHAVE ITALIC EMPIRE SURETY
Answer: What a tailgater is—A BUMPER STICKER

168. **Jumbles:** PONDER SUBTLY WEAPON UNSEAT BROKER OBTUSE
Answer: What a man might try to do on the golf-course—"PUTT" AWAY HIS TROUBLES

169. **Jumbles:** TIMING HAUNCH PANTRY VOYAGE PLACID TYCOON
Answer: What the cartographer was—CAUGHT MAPPING

170. **Jumbles:** CORNER TALKER BOUNTY IMPUTE PAUNCH UPKEEP
Answer: An usherette should know how to do this—PUT A MAN IN HIS PLACE

171. **Jumbles:** URCHIN SKEWER VALISE FAIRLY JERSEY POETIC
Answer: What inflation means—A CRISIS IN PRICES

172. **Jumbles:** DOMINO OUTLAW INWARD USEFUL MIDDAY AFFRAY
Answer: What a sheepskin is intended to keep—THE WOLF AWAY FROM THE DOOR

173. **Jumbles:** MOTHER ABRUPT UPSHOT HEIFER INTAKE JOSTLE
Answer: If you want to lose weight, don't talk about it—just do this—KEEP YOUR MOUTH SHUT

174. **Jumbles:** FIZZLE PIRACY DARING GHETTO FACTOR JACKAL
Answer: When the bride and groom start quarreling, it must have been this—AN "ALTAR-CATION"

175. **Jumbles:** HELIUM GROUCH EMBALM FASTEN INDOOR JANGLE
Answer: What a used car often is—NOT WHAT IT USED TO BE

176. **Jumbles:** CHORUS FIGURE DILUTE PROFIT IMPOSE ABUSED
Answer: What kind of a game is football?—A ROUGH & FUMBLE ONE

177. **Jumbles:** JABBER ALWAYS HINDER GUITAR DAHLIA ADVICE
Answer: What clothes make a woman—"DEAR" TO HER HUSBAND

178. **Jumbles:** DISMAY ANYONE FORAGE BUMPER SINFUL CRAFTY
Answer: What that clever miser was—A MAN OF RARE GIFTS

179. **Jumbles:** KERNEL GASKET AFLOAT IMBIBE CLUMSY PREACH
Answer: What a good weatherman is supposed to be—A STORM "SCENTER"

180. **Jumbles:** PLAGUE BALLAD LEGACY GOODLY BEWARE INVEST
Answer: Why the heirs were not surprised when the will was read—IT WAS A DEAD GIVEAWAY

Need More Jumbles®?

Jumble® Books

More than 175 puzzles each!

Cowboy Jumble®
ISBN: 978-1-62937-355-3

Jammin' Jumble®
ISBN: 1-57243-844-4

Java Jumble®
ISBN: 978-1-60078-415-6

Jazzy Jumble®
ISBN: 978-1-57243-962-7

Jet Set Jumble®
ISBN: 978-1-60078-353-1

Joyful Jumble®
ISBN: 978-1-60078-079-0

Juke Joint Jumble®
ISBN: 978-1-60078-295-4

Jumble® Anniversary
ISBN: 987-1-62937-734-6

Jumble® at Work
ISBN: 1-57243-147-4

Jumble® Ballet
ISBN: 978-1-62937-616-5

Jumble® Birthday
ISBN: 978-1-62937-652-3

Jumble® Celebration
ISBN: 978-1-60078-134-6

Jumble® Circus
ISBN: 978-1-60078-739-3

Jumble® Cuisine
ISBN: 978-1-62937-735-3

Jumble® Drag Race
ISBN: 978-1-62937-483-3

Jumble® Ever After
ISBN: 978-1-62937-785-8

Jumble® Explorer
ISBN: 978-1-60078-854-3

Jumble® Explosion
ISBN: 978-1-60078-078-3

Jumble® Fever
ISBN: 1-57243-593-3

Jumble® Fiesta
ISBN: 1-57243-626-3

Jumble® Fun
ISBN: 1-57243-379-5

Jumble® Galaxy
ISBN: 978-1-60078-583-2

Jumble® Garden
ISBN: 978-1-62937-653-0

Jumble® Genius
ISBN: 1-57243-896-7

Jumble® Geography
ISBN: 978-1-62937-615-8

Jumble® Getaway
ISBN: 978-1-60078-547-4

Jumble® Gold
ISBN: 978-1-62937-354-6

Jumble® Grab Bag
ISBN: 1-57243-273-X

Jumble® Gymnastics
ISBN: 978-1-62937-306-5

Jumble® Jackpot
ISBN: 1-57243-897-5

Jumble® Jailbreak
ISBN: 978-1-62937-002-6

Jumble® Jambalaya
ISBN: 978-1-60078-294-7

Jumble® Jamboree
ISBN: 1-57243-696-4

Jumble® Jitterbug
ISBN: 978-1-60078-584-9

Jumble® Journey
ISBN: 978-1-62937-549-6

Jumble® Jubilation
ISBN: 978-1-62937-784-1

Jumble® Jubilee
ISBN: 1-57243-231-4

Jumble® Juggernaut
ISBN: 978-1-60078-026-4

Jumble® Junction
ISBN: 1-57243-380-9

Jumble® Jungle
ISBN: 978-1-57243-961-0

Jumble® Kingdom
ISBN: 978-1-62937-079-8

Jumble® Knockout
ISBN: 978-1-62937-078-1

Jumble® Madness
ISBN: 1-892049-24-4

Jumble® Magic
ISBN: 978-1-60078-795-9

Jumble® Marathon
ISBN: 978-1-60078-944-1

Jumble® Neighbor
ISBN: 978-1-62937-845-9

Jumble® Parachute
ISBN: 978-1-62937-548-9

Jumble® Safari
ISBN: 978-1-60078-675-4

Jumble® See & Search
ISBN: 1-57243-549-6

Jumble® See & Search 2
ISBN: 1-57243-734-0

Jumble® Sensation
ISBN: 978-1-60078-548-1

Jumble® Surprise
ISBN: 1-57243-320-5

Jumble® Symphony
ISBN: 978-1-62937-131-3

Jumble® Theater
ISBN: 978-1-62937-484-03

Jumble® University
ISBN: 978-1-62937-001-9

Jumble® Unleashed
ISBN: 978-1-62937-844-2

Jumble® Vacation
ISBN: 978-1-60078-796-6

Jumble® Wedding
ISBN: 978-1-62937-307-2

Jumble® Workout
ISBN: 978-1-60078-943-4

Jumpin' Jumble®
ISBN: 978-1-60078-027-1

Lunar Jumble®
ISBN: 978-1-60078-853-6

Monster Jumble®
ISBN: 978-1-62937-213-6

Mystic Jumble®
ISBN: 978-1-62937-130-6

Outer Space Jumble®
ISBN: 978-1-60078-416-3

Rainy Day Jumble®
ISBN: 978-1-60078-352-4

Ready, Set, Jumble®
ISBN: 978-1-60078-133-0

Rock 'n' Roll Jumble®
ISBN: 978-1-60078-674-7

Royal Jumble®
ISBN: 978-1-60078-738-6

Sports Jumble®
ISBN: 1-57243-113-X

Summer Fun Jumble®
ISBN: 1-57243-114-8

Touchdown Jumble®
ISBN: 978-1-62937-212-9

Travel Jumble®
ISBN: 1-57243-198-9

TV Jumble®
ISBN: 1-57243-461-9

Oversize Jumble® Books

More than 500 puzzles each!

Generous Jumble®
ISBN: 1-57243-385-X

Giant Jumble®
ISBN: 1-57243-349-3

Gigantic Jumble®
ISBN: 1-57243-426-0

Jumbo Jumble®
ISBN: 1-57243-314-0

The Very Best of Jumble® BrainBusters
ISBN: 1-57243-845-2

Jumble® Crosswords™

More than 175 puzzles each!

More Jumble® Crosswords™
ISBN: 1-57243-386-8

Jumble® Crosswords™ Jackpot
ISBN: 1-57243-615-8

Jumble® Crosswords™ Jamboree
ISBN: 1-57243-787-1

Jumble® BrainBusters™

More than 175 puzzles each!

Jumble® BrainBusters™
ISBN: 1-892049-28-7

Jumble® BrainBusters™ II
ISBN: 1-57243-424-4

Jumble® BrainBusters™ III
ISBN: 1-57243-463-5

Jumble® BrainBusters™ IV
ISBN: 1-57243-489-9

Jumble® BrainBusters™ 5
ISBN: 1-57243-548-8

Jumble® BrainBusters™ Bonanza
ISBN: 1-57243-616-6

Boggle™ BrainBusters™
ISBN: 1-57243-592-5

Boggle™ BrainBusters™ 2
ISBN: 1-57243-788-X

Jumble® BrainBusters™ Junior
ISBN: 1-892049-29-5

Jumble® BrainBusters™ Junior II
ISBN: 1-57243-425-2

Fun in the Sun with Jumble® BrainBusters™
ISBN: 1-57243-733-2